SQL Introduction

USING

SQL Server 2022

Carsten Saastamoinen-Jakobsen

Preface

SQL – Structured Query Language – is a standard language for defining and manipulating objects and data in a relational database. There are many implementations of the language and none of these comply with the standard completely. Only the basic constructions are the same in all implementations. Therefore, it is important to know which product and even which version of the product is being used. This book uses Microsoft SQL Server version 2022 syntax.

The purpose of the book is to introduce the essential functionalities in SQL, in order to be able to move on with the more advanced possibilities. Only when the basic concepts are known it is possible to learn the more advanced options. This knowledge could be learning about 'The 8 Algebra Operations' to write statements that give the correct result, but also a statement that performs as well as possible. Don't focus on saving a few milliseconds if it's a statement that is executed once an hour. The statements where a few milliseconds need to be saved often need to be optimized by a very experienced developer - it's not for beginners. Knowing the basics can help you ignore some of the statements that are posted over and over again on the web and are stated as essential. Consider whether these statements are important to you.

The first chapter is about defining a database and tables. It is important how the database and tables are defined, as this knowledge will be used when writing manipulation statements. What data type does the column have, is a column defined to have only unique values, either because a PRIMARY KEY or a UNIQUE constraint is defined, can a column be NULL, is a FOREIGN KEY defined between two tables, etc. If this knowledge is not used when writing statements, the result of a query can very easily be wrong, maybe not today, but maybe later. The performance may also not be as good as it could be.

In this book, the focus is primarily on the SELECT statement. Other statements are reviewed and used without knowledge of the details. When developing a SELECT statement, the focus should be as follows in order of priority.

1. The query must give the correct result in relation to the data currently available in the tables.
2. The result must be correct in relation to the data that may be in the tables tomorrow due to new inserts or updates.
3. Statements must be written in a way that makes them easy to maintain. This means that it is immediately understandable, and that the various functionalities are used correctly and as intended. But it also means that the many - well-intentioned - suggestions from the web must be evaluated before they are used, to be sure whether they are as smart as claimed.
4. The execution of the statement should be acceptable. Not as fast as possible, but fast enough for the purpose it is designed for. But never faster than it still gives a correct result. Solutions also appear on the web that perform very fast but do not necessarily always give the correct result.

Statements are often prepared based on business understanding and not based on how the tables are defined in the database. It is important to know if all Orders point to a Customer and if all Orders always have at least one OrderLine. Do all Customers have address information – this may not be the case if we use a standard system. Many standard systems have very few rules as they are used by many different companies. In one company, it is important that the customer have an address, as the products must be delivered. In another company, the customer collects the goods themselves, but must have an invoice. Maybe the company name is enough and the address is ignored. Therefore, no time is spent storing this information and next time the customer may have changed their address. The customer's address is therefore not mandatory information in many standard system. Perhaps an Order do not have a reference to a Customer, as an Order is only created so that the product can be picked up at a warehouse further down the street.

If we know how programs work, we know that the OrderHeader information must be inserted first for the system to generate the OrderID value. Then, data about an OrderLine can be inserted. But what happens if the OrderLine data is never inserted? This is of course a bug in the system, but there are bugs in all systems. What if all the OrderLine information for an OrderHeader is deleted, is the OrderHeader data still in the system? Of course a bug – again – but still a bug.

If the statement is written assuming that all Orders point to a Customer, the query will be incorrect the day an Order exists without a reference to a Customer, because that is now allowed in the domain but only in the used system. If we examine the data, we can see that all Orders refer to a Customer and write the query based on this knowledge. But what happens in two years when the domain rules change and we store Orders without reference to a Customer. The domain rule has changed, but no changes have been made to our system. Will changing such a simple rule cause all queries to be fixed? Absolutely not.

It can be important when writing a statement whether a column's data is defined to be unique. They are only unique if the column is defined with PRIMARY KEY or UNIQUE constraint. A PRIMARY KEY does not accept NULL, but for the UNIQUE constraint, it needs to be decided whether a row can accept NULL. In articles on the web, it is often pointed out that a UNIQUE column accepts NULL. But this is not true because we can define the column to be both UNIQUE and NOT NULL. If that is the case, then there is no difference between PRIMARY KEY and UNIQUE. A column's data type determines how an expression/calculation should be specified.

Knowing all these rules and specifications is important if the query is to return the correct result today and tomorrow. If the query is not prepared so that it is easy to understand, and if the various constructs are not used correctly, errors will occur when the query needs to be maintained! A 'smart' construction has been found by searching the web - but consider whether this construction is smart. Unfortunately, there are many examples of this type of construction not lasting long, as the apparently 'smart' way of solving a problem only works in special cases and only based on certain requirements for the definition of the tables used.

There are also many 'rules' that abound among developers because they were previously necessary for good performance or because it's easier to write. Perhaps these rules no longer apply, or they may just be valid or have been in effect in other database systems. For example, there are arguments that performance is much better if, instead of specifying COUNT (*), we specify COUNT (Primary Key) or COUNT (1). This is not the case for SQL Server's version of SQL and never has been. It may also be that this is no longer the case, but only provided a performance advantage in earlier versions. The argument that it is easier to write never holds up with modern editors!

Good performance is important, but it should never be at the expense of a correct result! Fast execution should be achieved by trying to prepare the statement in several different ways and then choosing the best performing one. Good performance is also achieved by understanding the database system's way of solving a task, using the best design principles, and avoiding including redundant specifications such as DISTINCT where it is not necessary. To achieve good performance, there must also often be indexes that can be used when the statement is executed.

After reviewing the definition, there is a chapter with the INSERT, DELETE, UPDATE, MERGE and TRUNCATE statements. The purpose of this is to understand what the various constraints/limitations in the definition have on data. By reversing these statements, it becomes clear what the different limitations have on data.

The SELECT statement is then reviewed in the following chapters, by reviewing the individual clauses that make up the statement. We look at join in FROM, the condition that can be used in WHERE and how to specify the Projection.

In addition, there are chapters dealing with GROUP BY ... HAVING and Sub-Select. Together with Sub-Select we look at CTE. Views are introduced because they are used by many companies to ensure that the join is performed correctly, that a calculation is performed the same way every time, ... The mathematical operators UNION, INTERSECT and EXCEPT are reviewed. With these operations it is also shown that a given operation can be performed in multiple ways, both in terms of correctness but also for performance. When we look at correctness we have to choose whether the result should be mathematically correct or domain correct.

As the last chapter in the book we look at some of the system functions because it is often necessary to use a function to get the correct result. Only the most commonly used functions are shown.

As mentioned, all the examples in the book are written in Microsoft SQL Server syntax, unless otherwise stated.

Content

Introduction

In his book the primary focus is on SELECT. The SELECT statement is more complex than the other SQL statements, because we in one SELECT statement can work with many tables at the same time. INSERT, UPDATE and DELETE is only modifying on table.

The statements are categorized in several ways. We have statements to define objects in the database. These are categorized as DataDefinitionLanguage (DDL) and are

    CREATE   **ALTER**   **DROP**

We have statements to manipulate data. These are sometimes divided into two categories, so SELECT has its own category DQL, where Q stands for Query. But in this book, the DataManipulationLanguage (DML) category consists of the following statements

    SELECT   **INSERT**   **UPDATE**   **DELETE**

To me, TRUNCATE is also a DML statement, but is often categorized as DDL. I categorize this statement as a DML because in SQL Server it can be used to delete all or only some of the rows in a table. Categorizing the statement as DDL may be the reason for some of the incorrect claims made about the behaviour of this statement. The categorization is explained by reviewing the TRUNCATE statement. We also have a MERGE statement, which combines INSERT, UPDATE, and DELETE into one statement.

The last category is DataControlLanguage (DCL). Grant access to execute the above statements are one of the essential functionalities in a database system. DCL is outside the scope of this book.

    GRANT   **REVOKE**

We will look more at how a statement is executed. There are discussions about whether the SELECT statement should be written with the clauses in a different order, e.g. with FROM first. Unfortunately, this is because there is a wrong perception of SQL. It is not a procedural programming language based on the order in which the individual clauses of the statement are written. In a procedural programming language, the individual operations are performed exactly in the order described. We can use procedural code in SQL, but only in very few situations. We need to focus on the fact that a SELECT statement is Declarative.

That the SELECT statement is a Declarative statement is very important to understand in order to ignore some of the claims that are repeatedly posted on the web. What does it mean that a statement is DECLARATIVE. All clauses specified in the statement is analysed and used when the execution plan is generated. SQL is based on the mathematics of Algebra and Calculus.

Think of a natural language where we can express exactly the same thing, but with different word order depending on who is expressing something. "We need a flute for breakfast. Would you like to go to the baker and buy one" or "Go down to the baker and buy a flute for breakfast" or "We need a flute. We can't have breakfast until we get one from the baker". Only when we have heard the whole sentence do we know that the action is to be taken now before breakfast and not after breakfast and that it is 'you' who is to do it. But the construction of the sentence makes no difference in the actions that are to be taken – take your shoes on, go to the bakery, buy a flute, come back, take your shoes off, have breakfast with me! You know that wearing shoes is not allowed in the home, so you know how to behave. But we don't express the action like in a recipe. In wintertime it is also necessary to wear a jacket but the person pick up the flutes knows that.

When we write a SELECT statement, we do not know how the database system solves the problem. The data can be read from a table, but maybe being read from an index - a covered index - which contains all the data we need. Since the index is smaller and therefore faster to use, this is used for the statement. From the example above, we don't know whether the person is taking the bike or are walking. Everyone is hungry, so maybe the person is running to the bakery - speed is important. But that is not stated in the sentences about buying the flutes.

It may also be that we in SELECT statements write that the returned data should be ordered, but since there is an index with data in the desired order, sorting is ignored, by reading data from the index. We cannot read data in parallel, which gives better performance, but must read data sequentially to preserve the order. But we write ORDER BY in our statement because it is a requirement for the data we want to return. If the index is dropped, the problem is maybe solved by reading data in parallel and then sorting the data. If we do not have an index, we can define one, if evaluation shows that it improves performance and performance is important - but still the same statement written in the same way. If performance is not important, we do not create the index.

When developing/designing SQL, it was decided that the SELECT syntax should be as follows.

```
SELECT
        FROM
        WHERE
        GROUP BY
        HAVING
        ORDER BY
```

But the decision about syntax could as well have been different. If the following syntax had been decided when the SQL language was designed, a different order would simply have to be learned. Perhaps other objections could then be raised. Therefore, the syntax is not a problem, but should simply be noted. Think of a paper form where it is determined what should be entered in the individual fields. This could be an application for renewal of a passport, where any previous passport number is entered first, then nationality, then first name, then last name, etc. If it were you who was designing the form, it would probably look different, but neither better nor worse. You could have chosen as the first fields the last name and then first name, ... and a previous passport number as one of the last fields on the form.

```
FROM
        WHERE
        GROUP BY
        HAVING
        SELECT
        ORDER BY
```

The employee processing the application looks at the entire form to verify that everything necessary has been completed. If an earlier passport number is provided, this may be looked up in a system to check for similarities between new and old data. It does not matter whether this number is listed first or last, as long as it is available. The employee knows where to find it. All information must be present before the employee can go on with processing the application.

We know from address information that this can be different. In Denmark we have Street + Street number and in other countries it is Street number + Street. The different rules are known and not a problem. If you walk to the address, you have to find the street before using the number regardless of the order of entry!

Of course, it could have been decided that it was free in which order the various clauses should be written. But this can cause maintenance problems, especially with a statement written in many lines, because a detail easy might be overlooked if statements are not written with some discipline. Think of a long text without paragraphs. The three following ways of typing a statement is allowed and will compile and execute without errors. A not very long statement, because only two tables are referenced and not twelve.

```
SELECT   Orderline.OrderID, Orderline.ProductID, Product.ProductName, Product.IndicativePrice, Orderline.Price   FROM dbo.Orderline
INNER JOIN dbo.Product ON Orderline.ProductID = Product.ProductID WHERE Product.ProductID BETWEEN 2000 AND 3000 AND
Product.IndicativePrice <> Orderline.Price AND Orderline.OrderID > 2500;
```

```
SELECT   Orderline.OrderID, Orderline.ProductID, Product.ProductName, Product.IndicativePrice, Orderline.Price
        FROM dbo.Orderline INNER JOIN dbo.Product ON Orderline.ProductID = Product.ProductID
        WHERE   Product.ProductID BETWEEN 2000 AND 3000 AND Product.IndicativePrice <> Orderline.Price AND Orderline.OrderID > 2500;
```

```
SELECT    Orderline.OrderID,
          Orderline.ProductID,
          Product.ProductName,
          Product.IndicativePrice,
          Orderline.Price
          FROM dbo.Orderline INNER JOIN dbo.Product        ON Orderline.ProductID = Product.ProductID
          WHERE    Product.ProductID BETWEEN 2000 AND 3000      AND
                   Product.IndicativePrice <> Orderline.Price    AND
                   Orderline.OrderID > 2500;
```

The last of the statements above hopefully shows that it is easier to get an overview of which columns we want in the result. It is also easy to see that we have three expressions in the WHERE clause - a condition on the Product table, one on the dbo.Orderline table and one that compares columns from both tables. The expressions are combined with AND in the WHERE clause and not with OR. Therefore, it is of great importance to have a standard for setting up a query both during development to ensure that all rules for the result are specified, but also when it is delivered to production for easier maintenance.

The following table is a brief description of the clauses in SELECT and gives an overview of what the intention of the individual clauses is and decided when the language was specified.

SELECT	List of the columns included in the result table.
FROM	The tables from which data is selected. At the same time, the conditions/rules that must be met when two tables are joined are specified.
WHERE	The selection condition that applies to the result.
GROUP BY	The columns that the selected data must be group by for adding aggregation in the result.
HAVING	Condition for a group for the row be included in the result
ORDER BY	The order of the rows in the result table.

The three statements below is showing a solution to the task

> Show Name, Address, Zipcode and City for Persons where Name is 'Jens Olsen' and City 'Copenhagen'

```
-- Statement 1
SELECT    Person.Name,
          Person.Address,
          Person.Zipcode,
          Zipinfo.City
          FROM dbo.Person INNER JOIN dbo.Zipinfo ON Person.Zipcode = Zipinfo.Zipcode
          WHERE    Person.Name = 'Jens Olsen'       AND
                   Zipinfo.City = 'Copenhagen';
```

The Statement 1 is the 'correct' statement. After SELECT, the wanted columns are listed. In FROM we have the two tables from which the data is selected and the join condition specified after ON. In WHERE it is stated that it is Jens Olsen living in Copenhagen who must be included in the result. Everything in the statement follows the intent of the individual clauses.

```
-- Statement 2
SELECT    Person.Name,
          Person.Address,
          Person.Zipcode,
          Zipinfo.City
          FROM dbo.Person INNER JOIN dbo.Zipinfo ON      Person.Zipcode = Zipinfo.Zipcode    AND
                                                         Person.Name = 'Jens Olsen'          AND
                                                         Zipinfo.City = 'Copenhagen';
```

In Statement 2, the selection condition is moved from WHERE to ON. The argument for this is that the number of rows is reduced before the two tables are joined and that the statement then performs faster. However, this is incorrect because for both Statements 1 and 2, the rows included in the Join operation are filtered when they are read, and subsequent filtering is not necessary.

The same applies to Statement 3, which is seen as an example of optimization, since it is clear that data from the two tables is filtered before the join operation. There is just no difference between the execution plan of this statement and the two above. Maybe just more confusing to read especially when the statement becomes larger with many tables and conditions and thus more confusing.

```sql
-- Statement 3
WITH Persondata
AS
(
SELECT      Name,
            Address,
            Zipcode
            FROM dbo.Person
            WHERE Name = 'Jens Olsen'
),
Zipdata
AS
(
SELECT      Zipcode,
            City
            FROM dbo.Zipinfo
            WHERE Zipinfo.City = 'Copenhagen'
)
SELECT      Persondata.Name,
            Persondata.Address,
            Persondata.Zipcode,
            Zipdata.City
            FROM Persondata INNER JOIN Zipdata ON Persondata.Zipcode = Zipdata.Zipcode;
```

The following applies to all three statements. If a usable index exists, it is used. If no index exists, the rows that are not to be used are filtered out when reading data from the table. This ensures the compiler/optimizer, as the Declarative statement is evaluated for all specifications before execution. If we do not have usable indexes, the execution may change the next time the statement is executed if the necessary/usable/optimal index is created. Therefore, optimization in this situation is not about writing the statement differently, but about ensuring that the best options in terms of indexes are available to the compiler/optimizer. Other optimization options exist, but are not discussed here.

If we have an index on the tables we can maybe Seek for data, which means that we only read the rows with the wanted value. Depending on the index it can as well be a Seek combined with a filter operation. If the condition is

```sql
Name = 'Jensen'      AND      Zipcode = 2000
```

and we use the composite index containing the three columns

```
Name, Address, Zipcode
```

we can Seek/read using the Name column - yellow - and then filter on the Zipcode column - red. The following sketch shows how it works. We start with the first row with Name = 'Jensen' and stop when we reach 'Karlsen'. We read more rows - all named 'Jensen' - than necessary for the task, but fewer than all the rows in the table. So we read 9 rows out of many to end up returning 3 rows.

Name	Address	Zipcode
...	...	...
Iversen	...	...
Jensen	Adelgade	1000
Jensen	Borgergade	1000
Jensen	Borgergade	2000
Jensen	Nygade	1000
Jensen	Strandvejen	1000
Jensen	Strandvejen	2000
Jensen	Strandvejen	4000
Jensen	Tranevej	2000
Karlsen	...	...
...	...	

If the order of the columns in the index is as following

Name, Zipcode, Address

we read fewer rows because we can Seek on both Name and Zipcode. We start with Jensen/2000 and stop reading when we reach the row Jensen/4000. Only some of the 'Jensen' rows are read but all rows read must be returned in the result. No filter operation is necessary. We read 3 rows and return 3 rows.

Name	Zipcode	Address
...	...	...
Jensen	1000	Nygade
Jensen	2000	Borgergade
Jensen	2000	Strandvejen
Jensen	2000	Tranevej
Jensen	4000	Strandvejen
...	...	

If we do not have an usable index the following sketch shows a Scan of all the rows in the table followed by a filter on both Name and Zipcode. We read many rows and return 3 rows.

Name	Address	Zipcode
Hansen	Torvet	5000
Iversen	Nygade	9000
Thomsen	Adelgade	8000
Olsen	Borgergade	1000
Jensen	Tranevej	2000
Olsen	Nygade	1000
Poulsen	Nygade	8000
Jensen	Strandvejen	1000
Jensen	Strandvejen	2000
Andersen	Strandvejen	4000
Jensen	Borgergade	2000
Jensen	Adelgade	1000
Knudsen	Strandvejen	7000
Jensen	Nygade	3000
Larsen	Strandgade	9000
Carlsen	Nygade	2000
Thomsen	Borgergade	2000
Davidsen	Adelgade	6000

Therefore, a Seek on the rows gives the best performance, a Seek combined with a filter is the second best, and a Scan of all rows in the table followed by a filter gives the worst performance. But SQL Server select the best approach for the execution plan.

The following sketches give an idea of how the statement can be executed with and without an index. The barrels indicate that data is read from the table or from an index. Rectangle indicates the processes that are performed for execution of the statement. It is not necessary to filter data after join, because only the wanted rows are joined. The thickness of the arrows indicates the amount of data.

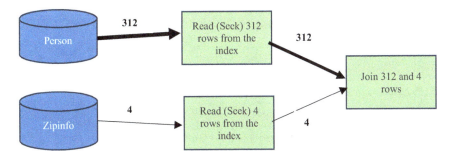

If we do not have indexes on the selection columns all rows from the table are read. This is called a SCAN operation of data. But the rows are filtered before the join operation is executed both for statement 1, 2 and 3 above.

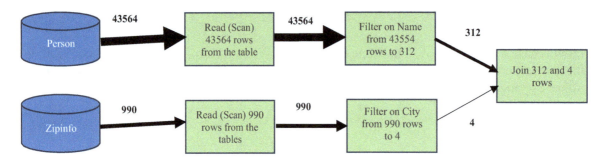

From the sketches above, we can conclude that it is not where we write the selection conditions that determines the performance. For both scenarios, we join 312 rows with 4 rows, and all result rows must be part of the final result. Therefore, no filter operation is necessary after joining.

Why this in an book about Introduction to SQL? Because many articles say that if we simply move the selection condition from xxx to yyy or use this zzz construct, the performance will be much better. But that is not correct. The statement is DECLARATIVE where we describe what the result should be, and not a procedural statement where we write how to get the correct result. That is the job of the compiler and the optimizer. It will even change over time because new indexes are defined or an index is changed or dropped.

We cannot cheat by writing the statement in an unintended way.

Different object types can be defined in a database. In the following there are sketches showing tables, Stored Procedure, View and use of a Sub-Select. A database can also contain Function, Index, Trigger, … but these object types are not described in this book. In a later chapter, we look at some of the System Functions that are important to be able to develop even simple statements.

dbo.Customer

CustomerID	Name	Adress	Zipcode
1453	Jens Olsen	Nygade 2	8000
285	Ida Jensen	Storegade 112	2000
4771	Steel Company	Strandvejen 4	4000
211	Frandsen aps	Vestergade 6	2000
1999	Johanne Lund	Nygade 23	4000

dbo.Zipinfo

Zipcode	City
2000	Frederiksberg
8000	Aarhus C
4000	Roskilde

dbo.OrderHeader

OrderID	OrderDate	CustomerID
20	2024-11-8	211
22	2024-11-15	4771
56	2024-12-3	211
99	2024-12-3	1999

dbo.OrderLine

OrderID	ProductID	NumberOfUnits	UnitPrice
20	1112	3	20.00
20	1122	4	43.50
22	1114	2	99.00
56	1112	2	20.00
56	1119	1	33.75
99	1113	9	10.00

```
CREATE PROCEDURE dbo.usp_Customer_Order
AS
SELECT     CustomerID,
           COUNT (*) AS NumberOfOrders
           FROM dbo.Customer INNER JOIN dbo.Orders
                ON Customer.CustomerID = Order.Customerid
           GROUP BY CustomerID;


CREATE VIEW dbo.CustomerData
AS
SELECT     Customer.CustomerID,
           Customer.Name,
           Customer.Street,
           Customer.Zipcode,
           Zipinfo.City
           FROM dbo.Customer INNER JOIN dbo.Zipinfo
                ON Customer.Zipcode = Zipinfo. Zipcode;


SELECT     OrderID,
           (SELECT COUNT (*) AS Number
                FROM dbo.OrderLine
                WHERE OrderLine.OrderID =
                      OrderHeader.OrderID) AS NumberLines
           FROM dbo.OrderHeader;


SELECT     ProductID
           FROM dbo.OrderLine
           WHERE UnitPrice < 30.00
UNION
SELECT     ProductID
           FROM dbo.OrderHeader INNER JOIN dbo.OrderLine
                ON OrderHeader.OrderID = OrderLine.OrderID
           WHERE OrderHeader.OrderDate = '2024-12-3';
```

In the following, we first look at the concept of the Relational Data Model. Then there is an overall review of the definition of a database and of the tables. We do not look at definition of Procedures and Functions.

To understand the meaning of the constraints/rules that can be defined for a table, we look at how data can be inserted and changed. The remaining chapters in the book deal with the SELECT statement.

Relational Data Model

A Relational Database is a data model that is based on mathematics and therefore uses many of the Mathematical concepts. In the Mathematics, the structure is Relations which in a Relational Database System is tables. We store data in tables, and the result from a SELECT statement is a table. The name Relational Database does not come from the fact that data in tables are related, but because the structure is Relations/tables.

When we look at a data model we have to look at and understand the following elements. A data model contains

- Data in a well-defined structure
- Implicit and explicit integrity rules
- Manipulation statements

A Relation consists of tuples. In the Relational Database Model, a table consists of rows. A tuple/row is an ordered set of values called the columns or attributes of the table. The allowed values for a column/attribute are defined by the domain of the column/attribute. The allowed values are in a database system, a data type specified for the column/attribute. The data type of the column/attribute can be combined with some restrictions on the values of the data type.

What are the implicit rules? These are the rules that come from the structure.

- All tuples/rows in a relation/table must have the same number of columns/attributes
- All values in a column/attribute must belong to the same domain

The explicit rules are the rules that can be defined for a given database/table. In the theory of database systems, there are various types of explicit integrity rules, i.e. rules that are specified for the column at the time of creation or later on and that must be complied when inserting, updating and deleting data. A distinction is made between 3 types

Domain integrity: The valid values in each column.
A column must always be specified with a data type. It will be possible to insert data into the column that does not comply with the domain rules, since the data type contains too many valid values in relation to the domain. It is therefore necessary to specify additional constraints in relation to the selected data type. This can be done, by defining a Check constraint or by using referential integrity rules.

Entity integrity: This rule specifies that all rows in a table must be unique.
This rule can be specified with the PRIMARY KEY and/or UNIQUE constraint.

Reference integrity: The value of a Foreign Keys column must exists as PRIMARY KEY/UNIQUE. The referential integrity rule states that all Foreign Key values must appear as a Primary Key or as a column with Unique values in the same table or in another table. Alternatively, the Foreign Key can be NULL. The rule is defined with FOREIGN KEY ... REFERENCES.

Database and Table

In this chapter there is an overview about how to create a database and how to add tables to the database.

Creating of a Database

A SQL Server instance always has at least four databases.

- master
- msdb
- tempdb
- model

In SQL Server we also have the hidden database Resource, but this is not mentioned in this book. The database master contains data about and references to all the other databases in the instance. In addition, it is also in this database error messages, System Stored Procedure, System Functions, System Views ... are stored. In the database msdb, information about the jobs to be performed on the server instance is stored. This could be a backup job. The database tempdb is important. When large tables are joined, there may not be enough memory to perform the operation. Therefore, tempdb is used as an intermediate storage. This can also be the case if a lot of data needs to be sorted. We can create own tables in tempdb, e.g. when evaluating different functionalities. In addition, it is possible to create temporary tables because it is necessary to be able to solve a specific task. The database model is a template for all new databases and contains all the system tables that must be in all new databases. Changes to the model database will only apply to all new subsequent databases.

When a custom database is created, it consists of at least one data file and one log file. The data file stores data from the various tables. In the log file information is stored about the changes that are continuously made to the data. To optimize it can be advantageous to create more data files for larger databases. The many details about this are beyond the scope of this book, as the main topics are about extracting data from an existing database/tables.

However, a few details are important. A database consists of at least one filegroup called PRIMARY. In this filegroup, all metadata for the database is stored in the system tables. In addition, multiple filegroups maybe containing multiple files can be defined. This is especially interesting in terms of Backup and Restore, but can also be crucial for performance if we work with large tables. The filegroups are the physical division of the database.

More interesting is it to look at the logical division of a database into several schemas. All databases are born with the schema dbo. If a database must contain tables for an insurance company, a table must be defined for each type of insurance. Since there are both policies and claims for motor vehicle insurance, life insurance and private insurance, etc., the database is divided into a schema for each type. A user can be assigned rights to a schema. This will be important and the most manageable if the system has several hundred tables, Stored Procedure, View, ... It may be important if an employee in the company only has rights to the data that relates to own area of expertise.

A simple database where a copy of the model database is made can be defined with the following statement, where neither data nor log file is specified. Information about this files is taken from the model database. If we need to create a database for evaluating a functionality, we can create our own database, if possible. Some developers use the tempdb database, but when using own defined database we can control when data is created, deleted, and modified and even take a backup for later use.

```
CREATE DATABASE TestDB;
```

If we want that the filegroup PRIMARY only contain the system tables we can create another filegroup – in the example named Userdata – used for storing user defined tables. This is the recommendation from Microsoft. We can specify that this filegroup is the default filegroup.

```
CREATE DATABASE TestDB
ON PRIMARY
(        NAME = N'TestDB',
         FILENAME = N'C:\Databases\TestDB.mdf',
         SIZE = 1024KB,
         MAXSIZE = UNLIMITED,
         FILEGROWTH = 1024KB
),
FILEGROUP UserData
(        NAME = N'TestDB_Userdata',
         FILENAME = N'C:\Databases\TestDB_Userdata.mdf',
         SIZE = 8192KB,
         MAXSIZE = UNLIMITED,
         FILEGROWTH = 8192KB
)
LOG ON
(        NAME = N'TestDB_log',
         FILENAME = N'D:\Logdata\TestDB_log.ldf',
         SIZE = 8192KB,
         MAXSIZE = UNLIMITED,
         FILEGROWTH = 8192KB
);
```

When we change the structures or the data in the tables, the changes are logged in the database log. When we change data, BeforeImage and AfterImage are stored. As the name suggests, BeforeImage contains data before the changes and AfterImage contains what the data looks like after the operation. In outline form, it looks like the following table. Other information stored in the log is ignored at this introductory level.

We are looking at the table dbo.Zipinfo with the three columns Zipcode, City and RegionID. The numbers 211, 288 and 471 are transaction numbers, so we can restore from the log in the right order and be sure that we match the BeforeImage and AfterImage from the same operation.

	Statement	BeforeImage	AfterImage
1	INSERT INTO dbo.Zipinfo (Zipcode, City, RegionID) VALUES (5000, 'Odense', 3);		211, 5000, Odense, 3
2	UPDATE dbo.Zipinfo SET City = 'Odense C' WHERE Zipcode = 5000;	288, 5000, Odense, 3	288, 5000, Odense C, 3
3	DELETE FROM dbo.Zipinfo WHERE Zipcode = 5000;	471, 5000, Odense C, 3	

If we want to restore data, we start by restoring a backup of the database. Then we can use the backup of the LOG to restore all changes since the database backup was taken and up until the crash. We can see from the first row in the sketch that it is an INSERT because we only have an AfterImage. There is no data before the operation is performed because we have no BeforeImage data, so the row <5000, Odense, 3> is an INSERT.

If we look at the second row from the Log backup, we can see that the old row <5000, Odense, 3> is changed/updated to <5000, Odense C, 3>. It is the log information for an UPDATE operation.

For the last row in the sketch, we only have a BeforeImage. There is no AfterImage and therefore no data after the operation is performed. The row <5000, Odense C, 3> is deleted as the result of a DELETE operation. If the used backup was from before performing the DELETE operation we can now remove the row using the Log data.

If we perform a ROLLBACK of a transaction where some changes have already been saved, we can use the Log data in reverse order. We can insert the row <5000, Odense C, 3> again, because it was an domain 'error' that the row was deleted. We change the row <5000, Odense C, 3> back to <5000, Odense, 3>. The UPDATE should never have been executed. Finally, we can delete the row from row number one in the sketch <5000, Odense, 3>.

Hope this small introduction to LOG and log data gives an insight into why it is important to care about the log. It is important to distinguish between RESTORE and ROLLBACK. With RESTORE we use a backup and add the changes that have been made since the used backup was created. This will often be many transactions.

With ROLLBACK we can undo the changes made in the current transaction. If a transaction has been completed with COMMIT, ROLLBACK cannot be performed, as other changes to the same data may have been made after COMMIT.

Next we will look at how we can create a table. The table and the columns must be giving a name. The names of the database's objects are called identifiers. An identifier must

- Start with a letter
- Be followed by a combination of letters, numbers, or _/underscore.

The following names are valid.

Customer	OrderHeader	Employee
CustomerID	customer_firstname	CustomerLastname

A standard should be created for how identifiers are named. Some prefer to use CamelCase, where every word in a compound word starts with a capital letter as in OrderLine and ProductName. Others separate words in a compound word with underscores. An example of this is order_line and product_name. Whether one standard or the other is chosen is not crucial, as long as it is the same principle that is applied consistently in a system.

If there are spaces in the name or the name consists of characters that do not comply with the above rules, the name must be delimited by quotation marks (") or brackets ([ ]). This also applies if reserved words are used as identifiers. Reserved words are those words that have a specific meaning in the language.

The following names are not valid

Customer number	123abc	Select

and must therefore be stated as

[Customer number] or "Customer number"	[123abc] or "123abc"	[Select] or "Select"

Use names so that they do not have to be separated by quotation marks or brackets. It can make the SQL statements less readable. The editor in SSMS also helps with coloured words, but this will not be the case if the name is given in brackets/square brackets.

```
CREATE TABLE dbo.Customer
(
        CustomerID        INT              NOT NULL
                          CONSTRAINT PK_Customer PRIMARY KEY,
        CustomerName      VARCHAR (35)     NOT NULL
);

CREATE TABLE dbo.[Customer data]
(
        [Primary Key]     [INT]            NOT NULL
                          CONSTRAINT PK_Customer_data PRIMARY KEY,
        [Customer Name]   [VARCHAR] (35)   NOT NULL
);
```

When querying the table the brackets are not shown.

```
SELECT    *
        FROM dbo.[Customer data];
```

Primary Key	Customer Name

Creating of a Table

Before we create a table, we need to know which columns are to be included in the table and which data types we want to use for the individual columns. We also need to know if there should be any restrictions/constraints defined on the individual columns.

We will first look at the data types that can be used. In SQL Server there are many data types, but some of them are seldom used. This is data types as XML, geographic, … We will only look at the most used.

Data Types

When a data type is to be specified, it is important that the correct data type is selected. But what is the correct data type? In any case, it is the most limiting in relation to the column's domain – valid values. It should take up as little space as possible in terms of the number of bytes.

A data type is characterized by the two properties that must be taken into account when choosing a data type.

- The valid values allowed for the data type.
- The operations that can be performed on data with the data type.

For the integer data type SMALLINT, the valid values are in the range from -32,768 to 32,767. Since it is a number, the operations are addition (+), multiplication (*), etc.

With standard systems, there can be problems, as the used data type often accept more values than we accept in our domain, or the data type is alphanumeric, where our valid values are numeric. It may also be that a string that allows too many characters.

Integers Data Types

SQL Server has 4 different integer data types. As seen from the following overview, SMALLINT, INT, and BIG-INT are signed integer data types, because they can contain both positive and negative numbers. An unsigned data type accepts only the positive numbers including 0.

We can add, subtract, multiply, divide, etc. 2 integers. It is the same operations that can be performed on all 4 data types, but the valid values are different. We must also pay attention to the data type for an intermediate result and the end result when calculating using the data type.

Data type	Storage	Values from	Values to
BIGINT	8 byte	-9.223.372.036.854.775.808	9.223.372.036.854.775.807
INT	4 byte	-2.147.483.648	2.147.483.647
SMALLINT	2 byte	-32.768	32.767
TINYINT	1 byte	0	255

When calculating SMALLINT values the data type of the intermediate result is a SMALLINT. If 25,000 is added to 20,000, the result will be 45,000. The expression fails because 45,000 is too large for valid values for the SMALLINT data type. One of the values must be converted to the data type INT with the function CAST. If an INT value is added to a SMALLINT value, the intermediate result will be INT and the result value 45,000 is valid for this data type. The expression does not fail.

String data types

There are both fixed length strings - the CHAR data type - and variable length strings - the VARCHAR data type. In SQL Server, the length can be from 1 up to 8000. If MAX is entered instead of an number, there can be up to 2GB of characters in the column. Always specify the length, as the default is 1.

```sql
CREATE TABLE dbo.t
(
        f1          CHAR (5),
        f2          CHAR (5)
);
GO
INSERT INTO dbo.t VALUES
        ('abc', 'ABC');
GO
DECLARE @c          CHAR (6);

SELECT      @c = f1 + f2
        FROM dbo.t;

SELECT @c;
```

Result
| abc..A |

Because the data type of f1 is fixed length, the column contains 'abc' with two trailing spaces after 'abc'. The result of concatenating f1 and f2 is 'abc..A', where the red dots shows spaces.

Variable length strings should be selected if the data is of variable length, such as Name and Address. For Customers, 40 characters will be enough for a column Name. The content of the column can then be used in different printouts without having to abbreviate the content. If it is the government's data on inhabitants of the country, there must be space for the full name, and then 40 characters is not enough. If strings are too long in relation to content, it can reduce performance.

NVARCHAR and NCHAR data types also exist. Each character occupies 2 bytes instead of 1 byte as for VARCHAR/CHAR. Therefore, the maximum length can only be 4000 characters and by specifying MAX, up to 1GB of characters can be inserted.

The N in NVARCHAR/NCHAR stands for National Character Set. This means that one row contains data with the Danish character set, another row with the French character set, etc.

Date and Time Data Types

In SQL Server, there are several data types that can be used for Date and Time data. If the column is to contain a date and/or time, one of the data types DATETIME, SMALLDATETIME, DATETIME2, DATE, or TIME can be used. In many systems, DATETIME or SMALLDATETIME is used, because DATETIME2, DATE and TIME were not introduced until version 2008. The DATETIME data type rounds the values to 3.3 milliseconds, which gives some problems. Before 2008, the DATETIME data type was used even though we only needed to store the date or the time.

```sql
CREATE TABLE dbo.t
(
        ID          INT          NOT NULL          IDENTITY
                    CONSTRAINT PK_t PRIMARY KEY,
        Date        DATETIME     NOT NULL
)
```

```
INSERT INTO dbo.t (Date) VALUES
        ('2024-3-22 23:59:59.996'),
        ('2024-3-22 23:59:59.997'),
        ('2024-3-22 23:59:59.998'),
        ('2024-3-22 23:59:59.999'),
        ('2024-3-23 00:00:00.000'),
        ('2024-3-23 00:00:00.001'),
        ('2024-3-23 00:00:00.002'),
        ('2024-3-23 00:00:00.003'),
        ('2024-3-23 00:00:00.004');
```

The following SELECT statement should intuitively produce a result with 2 rows, where the value in the first row is 4 because there are 4 rows for the day 2024-3-22. The value in the second row should be 5 because there are 5 rows where the day is 2024-3-23.

```
SELECT    COUNT (*)
          FROM dbo.t
          WHERE Date BETWEEN '2024-3-22 00:00:00.000' AND '2024-3-22 23:59:59.999'
UNION ALL
SELECT    COUNT (*)
          FROM dbo.t
          WHERE Date BETWEEN '2024-3-23 00:00:00.000' AND '2024-3-23 23:59:59.999';
```

If we look at the rows in the table, we can see that the data is rounded to the nearest 3 milliseconds, so the rows do not contain the values that are inserted and thus expected. The table contains the following data.

ID	Date
1	2024-03-22 23:59:59.997
2	2024-03-22 23:59:59.997
3	2024-03-22 23:59:59.997
4	2024-03-23 00:00:00.000
5	2024-03-23 00:00:00.000
6	2024-03-23 00:00:00.000
7	2024-03-23 00:00:00.003
8	2024-03-23 00:00:00.003
9	2024-03-23 00:00:00.003

The result from the SELECT statement shows that there are 6 rows where the day is 2024-3-22 and 6 rows for the day is 2024-3-23. So the result shows that the total number of rows is 12 even though there are only 9 rows in the table. For the BETWEEN condition both values specified are included.

The end date in the BETWEEN operator in the first SELECT statement - the value '2024-3-22 23:59:59.999' - will be rounded to '2024-3-23 00:00:00.000'. Therefore the rows with ID values 4, 5, and 6 are counted in both SELECT statements. So the correct statement should either be

```
SELECT    COUNT (*)
          FROM dbo.t
          WHERE Date BETWEEN '2024-3-22 00:00:00.000' AND '2024-3-22 23:59:59.997'
UNION ALL
SELECT    COUNT (*)
          FROM dbo.t
          WHERE Date BETWEEN '2024-3-23 00:00:00.000' AND '2024-3-23 23:59:59.997';
```

where the milliseconds of the first SELECT statement's end date are set to 997 to avoid rounding. Alternatively, the following statement will also ensure that there are no rows that are counted multiple times.

```
SELECT    COUNT (*)
          FROM dbo.t
          WHERE    Date >= '2024-3-22 00:00:00.000'          AND
                   Date < '2024-3-22 23:59:59.999'
UNION ALL
SELECT    COUNT(*)
          FROM dbo.t
          WHERE    Date >= '2024-3-23 00:00:00.000'          AND
                   Date < '2024-3-23 23:59:59.999';
```

The first of the 2 statements should not be used. If the statement needs to be changed, the person may mistakenly believe that it is an error that the entry is 997 and will change to 999 without thinking about the consequences. It can of course be learned, but is it told to all colleagues before the mistake happens.

We look at the difference using the data type DATETIME compared to the data type DATETIME2. If possible DATETIME2 should be used, because of no rounding problems.

With the following table and data we do not have the same problem as above. There are 7 decimal places specified. The number of decimal places can vary from 0 to 7, but without the problems of rounding.

```sql
CREATE TABLE dbo.t
(
        ID          INT                     NOT NULL IDENTITY
                    CONSTRAINT PK_t PRIMARY KEY,
        Date        DATETIME2 (7)           NOT NULL
);
GO
INSERT INTO dbo.t (Date) VALUES
        ('2024-3-22 23:59:59.9999996'),
        ('2024-3-22 23:59:59.9999997'),
        ('2024-3-22 23:59:59.9999998'),
        ('2024-3-22 23:59:59.9999999'),
        ('2024-3-23 00:00:00.0000000'),
        ('2024-3-23 00:00:00.0000001'),
        ('2024-3-23 00:00:00.0000002'),
        ('2024-3-23 00:00:00.0000003'),
        ('2024-3-23 00:00:00.0000004');
```

The following statement will give the result 4 for the date 2024-3-22 and 5 for the date 2024-3-23. A total of 9 rows, which is also the number of rows in the table.

```sql
SELECT    COUNT (*)
        FROM dbo.t
        WHERE Date BETWEEN '2024-3-22 00:00:00.0000000' AND '2024-3-22 23:59:59.9999999'
UNION ALL
SELECT    COUNT (*)
        FROM dbo.t
        WHERE Date BETWEEN '2024-3-23 00:00:00.0000000' AND '2024-3-23 23:59:59.9999997';
```

Decimal Data Types

With decimal data, we can choose between the data types DECIMAL, REAL, FLOAT and MONEY. DECIMAL is a precise data type where we can choose the number of decimal places, while the floating data types REAL and FLOAT are not precise, but approximate data types. Money is a predefined data type with four decimal places. The values in the floating point data type aren't accurate. It must be considered how an expression with operators with the same precedence is written.

```sql
CREATE TABLE dbo.t
(
        RealValue               REAL
);
GO
INSERT INTO dbo.t VALUES
        (123456789),
        (987654321);

SELECT    RealValue                       AS Column1,
        RealValue + 124                   AS Column2,
        124 + RealValue                   AS Column3,
        RealValue + 31 + 31 + 31          AS Column4,
        31 + 31 + 31 + RealValue          AS Column5
        FROM dbo.t;
```

Column1	Column2	Column3	Column4	Column5
1.234568E+08	1.234569E+08	1.234569E+08	1.234569E+08	1.234569E+08
9.876543E+08	9.876545E+08	9.876545E+08	9.876543E+08	9.876545E+08

We can see for the first row, that the calculated value in columns Column2, Column3, Column4 and Column5 have the same value. But for the second row, Column4 differs from the others. If we add 31 even more times for Column4, the result will still be the same, as a rounding is done after each calculation. The column Column5 has the same value as the columns Column2 and Column3. The expression is calculated from left to right, so the 4 times 31 given at the beginning is added to 124 before being added to the value of the RealValue column.

If the floating point data type is used, a standard should be defined for how an expression is calculated in the company. This can be crucial if a percentage calculation of VAT or duties is to be made. The following formulas are both mathematically correct, but may give different results.

Amount / 100 * VatPct	Amount * VatPct / 100

If we have a column Amount defined with the data type REAL, and 106.00 is inserted into the column, the two following statements will give different results. The first statement will return one row, but the second statement will return the empty table.

```
SELECT   *
         FROM dbo.t
         WHERE Amount * 25 / 100 = 26.50;

SELECT   *
         FROM dbo.t
         WHERE Amount / 100 * 25 = 26.50;
```

If the calculated value is rounded to 6 decimal places the result values are different.

```
SELECT   ROUND (Amount * 25 / 100, 6)   AS Amount1,
         ROUND (Amount / 100 * 25, 6)   AS Amount2
         FROM dbo.t;
```

Amount1	Amount2
26.5	26.499998

For the DECIMAL data type, it is specified how many digits should occur in total and how many of these should be decimals.

```
Amount              DECIMAL (9,2)
```

If we execute the above statement with this definition of the Amount column, both formulas will result in the same value.

Amount1	Amount2
26.500000	26.500000

The DECIMAL data type is an exact data type, so when used, there are not the same problems with the calculation order as shown for the floating-point data type.

Bit Data Type

If columns with the data type BIT are used, the column can be assigned the value 0 or 1. In addition, the column can be NULL. However, there is a special rule for this data type that if a numeric value is inserted different from 0 or 1, the value is converted to 1. We do not have the keywords true and false but can assign the string values 'True' and 'False' to a bit. The string values are not case sensitive.

Constraints

The following shows some CREATE TABLE statements. It is an overall review of the various options and what this means both in terms of advantages and disadvantages. We are looking at the following constraints.

- Primary Key
  - All values are unique and the column must also be defined with NOT NULL. Only one Primary Key is allowed for each table.
- Unique
  - All values are unique. If the column allows NULL only one row can be NULL. Many Unique constraints can be specified for each table.
- Check
  - Simple expressions can be specified to reduce the allowed values from the legal values of the data type. In SQL Server, a Sub-Select is not allowed.
- Foreign Key
  - Reference a PRIMARY KEY/UNIQUE column in another table or in the same table, The FOREIGN KEY can be composite of several columns. The FOREIGN KEY column can be NULL.
- NULL / NOT NULL.
  - For me NULL is not a value. I use the word 'NULL' and not 'NULL value'.

All constraints in the following are given a name with the exception of NULL/NOT NULL. If the constraints are not explicitly assigned a name, the database system will form a name. The name must be used, if the rule is to be changed or removed. Define a standard for how this naming should be. It is important to specify a meaningful name both for understanding the constraint without going into details but also for 'remembering' to change all the constraints if the domain rules need to be changed. In this book, the following standard is used. The name is also shown in an error message.

PRIMARY KEY	PK_tablename
UNIQUE	UQ_tablename_columnname. If the unique information is composed of multiple columns then UQ_tablename_columnname1_columnname2
CHECK	CK_tablename_columnname If the condition refers to multiple columns then CK_tablename_columnname1_columnname2
FOREIGN KEY	FK_fktablename_uqtablename If there are multiple Foreign Keys between two tables, the column name or role is added

In the following example, we look at some tables for storing data about a Product. I always specify both schema and table name. Let's look at the dbo.Category table.

```
CREATE TABLE dbo.Category
(
        CategoryID        SMALLINT        NOT NULL
                          CONSTRAINT PK_Category PRIMARY KEY,
        CategoryName      VARCHAR (30)    NOT NULL
);
```

The table dbo.Category contains 2 columns. The CategoryID columns have the data type SMALLINT, which means that the valid values for the column can be between -32,768 and 32,767. CategoryID must be a negative number but the values in the column must be unique, as the column is the table's PRIMARY KEY. The column CategoryName have no constraints defined so several categories can have the same CategoryName. The column CategoryName must be defined with a UNIQUE constraint if the values in the column must be unique.

The next table is the dbo.Product table. Several different constraints are defined for this table.

```
CREATE TABLE dbo.Product
(
        ProductID           INT             NOT NULL
                            CONSTRAINT PK_Product PRIMARY KEY,
```

```
        ProductName        VARCHAR (30)      NOT NULL
                           CONSTRAINT UQ_Product_ProductName UNIQUE,
        UnitInStore        SMALLINT          NOT NULL DEFAULT (0)
                           CONSTRAINT CK_Product_UnitInStore CHECK (UnitInStore >= 0),
        IndicativePrice    DECIMAL (9,2)     NOT NULL
                           CONSTRAINT CK_Product_IndicativePrice CHECK(IndicativePrice >= 0),
        CategoryID         SMALLINT          NOT NULL
                           CONSTRAINT FK_Product_Category FOREIGN KEY REFERENCES dbo.Category (CategoryID),
        ProductCreated     DATE              NOT NULL
                           CONSTRAINT DF_Product_ProductCreated DEFAULT (SYSDATETIME ()),
        ProductChanged     DATE              NULL
);
```

The columns UnitInStore and IndicativePrice must have a value that is zero or is a positive value. The allowed values of the specified data types have been limited to only be the positive values or 0.

When inserting a new product, UnitInStore must have a value. If the column is not included in the INSERT statement, the default value 0 is used. If no DEFAULT constraint is defined, the column will be NULL.

The value for the CategoryID column must be a value that already exists as CategoryID in the dbo.Category table. The FOREIGN KEY constraint is defined. If the CategoryID in the Category table is referenced from dbo.Product it cannot be deleted or changed having a new CategoryID value in the dbo.Category table. It is important that a column with a FOREIGN KEY constraint defined can be specified to accept NULL. When the column is NULL, there is no evaluation for whether the value is legal. We do not need to have a NULL in the dbo.Category table.

It can be inferred from the definition that a row that has not changed will have NULL in the ProductChanged column. But for the developer of the table, the idea was that only changes in one of the columns ProductName, CategoryID or IndicativePrice should result in a new value in ProductChanged. If the UnitInStore is changed, the value in the ProductChanged column is not changed. It will be changed too often and may not have any useful value. This cannot be read out of the definition. Be careful not to conclude that there is a rule that does not apply.

The following shows the definition of the dbo.Zipinfo table, where the PRIMARY KEY is a surrogate key.

```
CREATE TABLE dbo.Zipinfo
(
        ZipSerialNo        INT               NOT NULL
                           CONSTRAINT PK_Zipinfo PRIMARY KEY,
        Zipcode            SMALLINT          NOT NULL
                           CONSTRAINT UQ_Zipinfo_Zipcode UNIQUE,
        City               VARCHAR (20)      NOT NULL
);
```

Since a value for Zipcode must only occur once in the table, this column is defined with the UNIQUE constraint. By using this principle, you can change the value of a Zipcode without having to change values in the tables where the value is referenced. The same City name may well occur several times in the table.

In the dbo.Employee table the IDENTITY is specified.

```
CREATE TABLE dbo.Employee
(
        EmployeeID         INT      NOT NULL           IDENTITY
                           CONSTRAINT PK_Employee PRIMARY KEY,
...
);
```

In the dbo.Employee table, the EmployeeID column is the PRIMARY KEY. The column is automatically assigned a value when a new row is inserted. This is specified with the IDENTITY keyword. It is important to note that this does not mean that all values are consecutive, even though no row has been deleted in the table. If we try to insert a row but the insertion fails due to an error in one of the columns, the IDENTITY value will already be selected and is therefore used. When the error is corrected and the row is inserted without error, a new IDENTITY value is selected.

In the table dbo.Order we look at the CHECK constraint.

```sql
CREATE TABLE dbo.OrderHeader
(
        OrderID         INT     NOT NULL
                        CONSTRAINT PK_Order PRIMARY KEY,
        OrderDate       DATE    NOT NULL DEFAULT (SYSDATETIME ()),
        DeliveryDate    DATE    NULL,
        PaymentDate     DATE    NULL,
        CustomerID      INT     NULL,
        CONSTRAINT CK_Order_DeliveryDate CHECK (DeliveryDate >= OrderDate),
        CONSTRAINT CK_Order_PaymentDate CHECK (PaymentDate >= DeliveryDate)
);
```

The OrderDate column must always have a value. By default, the column will be stamped with today's date. If a value is specified for the DeliveryDate column, it must be greater than or equal to the OrderDate value. The PaymentDate must be greater than or equal to the DeliveryDate.

DeliveryDate and PaymentDate can be NULL. NULL can indicate that the Order has not yet been delivered or not yet paid. The columns get a value when they change state to Delivered and to Paid. In some systems you may find that a value is specified instead. This can be '1753-1-1', '1900-1-1', '2099-12-31' or '9999-12-31'. These are the most commonly used dates instead of NULL. Other values may be used. If NULL is not used for a Date column, you need to find out which date value is used instead. In some systems, several different values may unfortunately be used. Both earlier and later date values are used in various systems as a replacement value for NULL.

The conclusion of the above is that it is important to know the data type of a column and whether the column is defined to accept NULL or whether all rows must have a value for the column but some of the values are replacement values for NULL. It is important to know exactly all the constraints that are defined on a table.

Information about constraints on user-defined tables is stored in system tables and can be queried using the following statement. The columns type and type_desc shows the type of constraint/information.

C	Check constraint
D	Default
F	Foreign key constraint
PK	Primary key constraint
UQ	Unique constraint

```sql
SELECT  *
        FROM sys.objects;
```

Some views have been defined so that it is possible to query the data of a special type.

The sys.tables view shows which user defined tables exist in a database. In the following statement, some of the columns are shown.

```sql
SELECT  name,
        object_id,
        type_desc,
        create_date,
        modify_date
        FROM sys.tables;
```

If we want to select if any columns is defined to be unique the sys.key_constraints shows both PRIMARY KEY and UNIQUE constraints.

```sql
SELECT  *
        FROM sys.key_constraints
        WHERE parent_object_id = OBJECT_ID ('Employee');
```

It can be important to know if FOREIGN KEY is defined. Both the system tables sys.foreign_keys and sys.foreign_key_columns can be used. If the constraints are named appropriately, the name may tell which columns the

FOREIGN KEY is defined for, else the result from sys.foreign_key_columns must be used. The column_id values can be used in the result from sys.columns for information about the columns name, data type, nullability, etc.

```sql
SELECT   *
    FROM sys.foreign_keys
    WHERE parent_object_id = OBJECT_ID ('Employee');

SELECT   *
    FROM sys.foreign_key_columns
    WHERE parent_object_id = OBJECT_ID ('Employee');
```

The sys.check_constraints view shows information about CHECK constraints,

```sql
SELECT   *
    FROM sys.check_constraints
    WHERE parent_object_id = OBJECT_ID ('Employee');
```

Most interesting is maybe information about which DEFAULT values is defined.

```sql
SELECT   *
    FROM sys.default_constraints
    WHERE parent_object_id = OBJECT_ID ('Employee');
```

To select information about the individual columns in a table, FOREIGN KEY, … use the view sys.columns. The example shows data about the Employee table.

```sql
SELECT   object_id,
    name,
    column_id,
    system_type_id,
    max_length,
    precision,
    scale,
    default_object_id
    FROM sys.columns
    WHERE object_id = OBJECT_ID ('Employee');
```

All these views are interesting if we don't use a tool that can display this information. We can instead execute the above statements.

Change Data in the Tables

In this chapter we will look at INSERT, UPDATE and DELETE statements with details. But we also have an overview of TRUNCATE and MERGE because this statements can be found when maintaining statements developed by others.

When manipulating data, the statements should be included in a transaction. One of the many myths often repeated in articles on the Internet claims that a TRUNCATE operation cannot be rolled back. This is not correct. To demonstrate the principles, we evaluate using the INSERT statement combined with a user-defined transaction. The same principle applies to all the different manipulation statements. The table dbo.t is defined with the column ID as an IDENTITY column, which means that the column is an autonumber column which is assigned a value when inserting a new row. First we insert three rows.

```
CREATE TABLE dbo.t
(
        ID      INT     NOT NULL        IDENTITY
                CONSTRAINT PK_t PRIMARY KEY,
        f1      INT     NOT NULL
                CONSTRAINT CK_t_f1 CHECK (f1 BETWEEN 1 AND 100)
);
GO
INSERT INTO dbo.t (f1) VALUES
        (1),    (21),   (44);
```

ID	f1
1	1
2	21
3	44

The following INSERT will return an error and the table contains the same 3 rows.

```
INSERT INTO dbo.t (f1) VALUES
        (1000);
```

With the following INSERT statement the table dbo.t will contains 4 rows. The ID value for the new row is 5, because we 'lost' the IDENTITY value 4 when trying to insert 1000 into the column f1.

```
INSERT INTO dbo.t (f1) VALUES
        (77);
```

ID	f1
1	1
2	21
3	44
5	77

If the INSERT statement is executed in a user defined transaction, the IDENTITY value(s) are also 'lost' if ROLLBACK is executed.

We can break the sequence by specifying that the next number is specified in the INSERT statement.

```
SET IDENTITY_INSERT dbo.t ON;

INSERT INTO dbo.t (ID, f1) VALUES
        (32, 10);

SET IDENTITY_INSERT dbo.t OFF;
```

After execution we continue from this new value, so the next IDENTITY/ID value is 33. We can get errors if we break the rule that the ID column is PRIMARY KEY.

When we change data in one or more tables, we should specify a user-defined transaction. This can be used, for example, when creating a new Order. We need to insert one row into the OrderHeader table and at least one row into the OrderLine table. An Order without at least one OrderLine is not an Order in our domain. We start with BEGIN TRANSACTION and then start inserting the rows. If an error occurs, ROLLBACK TRANSACTION is executed and all rows inserted after BEGIN TRANSACTION are removed from the tables. We do not necessarily know how many rows have been inserted because inserting a row into the OrderHeader table may fail or maybe only when we insert 7 OrderLine rows where the last one fails. But the database system has information about this, as all changes are stored in the log file. If no errors occur, COMMIT TRANSACTION is executed and the Order is stored for the future.

In the sketch below, we use TRY ... CATCH. This statement will not be discussed in detail, but hopefully the following is understandable. If an error occurs while executing any of the statements in the TRY block, the statement under CATCH is executed. Otherwise, we just execute all the statements specified in the TRY block. For the example we use the following three tables. In the dbo.Product table we insert 4 rows.

```
CREATE TABLE dbo.Product
(
        ProductID           INT             NOT NULL
                            CONSTRAINT PK_Product PRIMARY KEY,
        ProductName         VARCHAR (20)    NOT NULL
);


CREATE TABLE dbo.OrderHeader
(
        OrderID             INT             NOT NULL
                            CONSTRAINT PK_OrderHeader PRIMARY KEY,
        OrderDate           DATE            NOT NULL
                            CONSTRAINT DF_OrderHeader_OrderDate DEFAULT (SYSDATETIME ())
);


CREATE TABLE dbo.OrderLine
(
        OrderID             INT             NOT NULL,
        ProductID           INT             NOT NULL
                            CONSTRAINT FK_OrderLine_Product REFERENCES dbo.Product (ProductID),
        NumberOfUnits       SMALLINT        NOT NULL
        CONSTRAINT PK_OrderLine PRIMARY KEY (OrderID, ProductID)
);
```

We do not specify a user-defined transaction, so the system therefore defines an implicit transaction.

```
INSERT INTO dbo.Product (ProductID, ProductName) VALUES
        (1, 'Product 1'),     (2, 'Product 2'),     (3, 'Product 3'),     (4, 'Product 4');
```

First we insert an Order with OrderID = 10 into the empty tables.

```
BEGIN TRY
        BEGIN TRANSACTION;

        INSERT INTO dbo.OrderHeader (OrderID) VALUES (10);

        INSERT INTO dbo.OrderLine (OrderID, ProductID, NumberOfUnits) VALUES (10, 2, 5);
        INSERT INTO dbo.OrderLine (OrderID, ProductID, NumberOfUnits) VALUES (10, 4, 1);

        COMMIT TRANSACTION;
END TRY
BEGIN CATCH
        ROLLBACK TRANSACTION;
END CATCH;
```

The Order is stored in the tables because the COMMIT TRANSACTION is executed. No errors occur and all the statements in the TRY block are executed. Then we insert the Order with OrderID = 11.

```
BEGIN TRY
        BEGIN TRANSACTION;

        INSERT INTO dbo.OrderHeader (OrderID) VALUES (11);
```

```
        INSERT INTO dbo.OrderLine (OrderID, ProductID, NumberOfUnits) VALUES (11, 3, 2);
        INSERT INTO dbo.OrderLine (OrderID, ProductID, NumberOfUnits) VALUES (11, 14, 1);

        COMMIT TRANSACTION;
END TRY
BEGIN CATCH
        ROLLBACK TRANSACTION;
END CATCH;
```

The dbo.OrderHeader row is inserted. Then the dbo.OrderLine with ProductID = 3 is inserted without any error. We try to insert the dbo.OrderLine with ProductID = 14, but this insert return an error, because ProductID = 14 do not exists and we have the FOREIGN KEY defined. The statement in the CATCH block is executed, and the dbo.OrderLine 11/3/2 and the dbo.OrderHeader 11 row is removed from the tables. No new rows are inserted.

Then we try to insert a new Order with OrderID = 10.

```
BEGIN TRY
        BEGIN TRANSACTION;

        INSERT INTO dbo.OrderHeader (OrderID) VALUES (10);
        INSERT INTO dbo.OrderLine (OrderID, ProductID, NumberOfUnits) VALUES (10, 1, 3);

        COMMIT TRANSACTION;
END TRY
BEGIN CATCH
        ROLLBACK TRANSACTION;
END CATCH;
```

When we try to insert the row in the table dbo.OrderHeader we get an error, because the OrderID column is PRIMARY KEY and a row with the value 10 already exists in the dbo.OrderHeader table. Therefore, ROLLBACK TRANSACTION is performed.

After trying to insert the Order with OrderID = 10, then the OrderID = 11 and again OrderID = 10 we end up with this rows in the tables.

SELECT * FROM dbo.OrderHeader;			SELECT * FROM dbo.OrderLine;		
OrderID	**OrderDate**		**OrderID**	**ProductID**	**NumberOfUnits**
10	2024-11-19		10	2	5
			10	4	1

With transactions not all domain rules can be controlled. We can insert a row into dbo.OrderHeader without inserting any row(s) in dbo.OrderLine. Of course a domain error but not a database error. But we cannot insert rows into the table dbo.OrderLine without a reference to dbo.OrderHeader rows. This will return a database error.

If we perform the following statements the row with value 55 is inserted. The statement ROLLBACK TRANSACTION return an error, because we do not have a matching BEGIN TRANSACTION. If we don't specify a custom transaction, each manipulation statement is wrapped in an implicit transaction. What is executed for the statement is shown to the right.

We type and execute	SQL Execute
INSERT INTO dbo.OrderHeader (OrderID) VALUES (55); ROLLBACK TRANSACTION;	BEGIN TRANSACTION; INSERT INTO dbo.OrderHeader (OrderID) VALUES (55); COMMIT TRANSACTION; ROLLBACK TRANSACTION;

The execution fail with the following error.

The ROLLBACK TRANSACTION request has no corresponding BEGIN TRANSACTION.

Because the transaction is already implicit committed, it is not possible to ROLLBACK TRANSACTION, and we get an error. The INSERT statement has already been committed and is therefore unaffected by the ROLLBACK

TRANSACTION statement. It is not possible to ROLLBACK after COMMIT or COMMIT after ROLLBACK. Either ROLLBACK or COMMIT is performed, but never both. The table has one more row.

If we INSERT several rows without having a user-defined transaction it is executed like the following.

We type and execute	SQL Execute

INSERT INTO dbo.OrderHeader VALUES (22, NULL);	BEGIN TRANSACTION;
	      INSERT INTO dbo.OrderHeader VALUES (22, NULL);
	COMMIT TRANSACTION;
	
	BEGIN TRANSACTION;
	      INSERT INTO dbo.OrderLine VALUES (22, 2, 2);
	COMMIT TRANSACTION;
	
	BEGIN TRANSACTION;
	      INSERT INTO dbo.OrderLine VALUES (22, 4, 1);
	COMMIT TRANSACTION;

INSERT INTO dbo.OrderLine VALUES (22, 2, 2); INSERT INTO dbo.OrderLine VALUES (22, 4, 1);	

With this script, the row in dbo.OrderHeader may be inserted, but one or both rows in dbo.OrderLine fail. In the following we execute the INSERT statement in a user-defined transaction. It is possible to evaluate before we decide to COMMIT or ROLLBACK.

```
BEGIN TRANSACTION;

INSERT INTO dbo.OrderHeader (OrderID) VALUES (10);

IF @@ERROR = 0
        COMMIT TRANSACTION
ELSE
        ROLLBACK TRANSACTION;
```

If the variable @@ERROR returns 0 no error has occurred.

INSERT

For INSERT, there are several options. One or more rows can be inserted into a table either by entering the values or by executing a SELECT statement. We use the following tables.

```
CREATE TABLE dbo.Zipinfo
(
        Zipcode             SMALLINT          NOT NULL
                            CONSTRAINT PK_Zipinfo PRIMARY KEY,
        City                VARCHAR (20)      NOT NULL
);


CREATE TABLE dbo.CustomerType
(
        CustomerTypeID      CHAR (1)          NOT NULL
                            CONSTRAINT PK_CustomerType PRIMARY KEY,
        CustomerTypeTxt     VARCHAR (20)      NOT NULL
                            CONSTRAINT UQ_CustomerType_CustomerTypeTxt UNIQUE

);


CREATE TABLE dbo.Customer
(
        CustomerID          INT               NOT NULL
                            CONSTRAINT PK_Customer PRIMARY KEY,
        Name                VARCHAR (35)      NOT NULL,
        Address             VARCHAR (35)      NULL,
        Zipcode             SMALLINT          NULL
                            CONSTRAINT FK_Customer_Zipinfo FOREIGN KEY REFERENCES dbo.Zipinfo (Zipcode),
        CustomerTypeID      CHAR (1)          NOT NULL
                            CONSTRAINT FK_Customer_CustomerType FOREIGN KEY REFERENCES dbo.CustomerType (CustomerTypeID),
);
```

Before inserting a new Customer, we need to insert data into dbo.Zipinfo and dbo.CustomerType tables because we have the FOREIGN KEY defined. First, we insert one row into dbo.Zipinfo. The column list is specified.

```sql
INSERT INTO dbo.Zipinfo (Zipcode, City) VALUES
        (2000, 'Frederiksberg');
```

It is possible to insert more than one row at a time. We use a table value constructor. It is important that if one of the rows results in an error, it is the statement that fails. So no rows - not even rows without errors - are inserted.

```sql
INSERT INTO dbo.Zipinfo (Zipcode, City) VALUES
        (5000, 'Odense'),            (8000, 'Aarhus C'),            (9000, 'Aalborg');
```

Because the column list is specified, we can enter the values in any order as long as it fits the column list.

```sql
INSERT INTO dbo.Zipinfo (City, Zipcode) VALUES
        ('Kolding', 6000);
```

The columns in a row are ordered. The following statement shows, that in the CustomerType table the column CustomerTypeID is the first column and CustomerTypeTxt the second column.

```sql
SELECT    name,
          column_id
        FROM sys.columns
        WHERE object_id = OBJECT_ID ('CustomerType');
```

name	column_id
CustomerTypeID	1
CustomerTypeTxt	2

Because of known ordering of columns, we can omit the column list in an INSERT statement, as long as the values are listed in the correct order relative to the order specified in the system tables. Never omit the column list in production systems, because a change to the table structure will hopefully cause an error in the INSERT statement if not fixed. Changing the table can be both deleting a column and inserting a new one, so that the number of values matches the number of columns. If we have a column list in the statement we will get an error, if we reference a column that not exist anymore in the table.

```sql
INSERT INTO dbo.CustomerType (CustomerTypeID, CustomerTypeTxt) VALUES
        ('C', 'Company'),            ('O', 'Ordinary'),            ('P', 'Public');
```

We look at the dbo.Customer table. With the first INSERT statement there are no problems. All columns are given a value and the values in the Zipcode and CustomerType columns are valid.

```sql
INSERT INTO dbo.Customer (CustomerID, Name, Address, Zipcode, CustomerTypeID) VALUES
        (1, 'John Olsson', 'Nygade 22', 2000, 'O');
```

The next INSERT statement is also correct. The columns Address and Zipcode allow NULL and are omitted both in the column and value list and therefore NULL in the row.

```sql
INSERT INTO dbo.Customer (CustomerID, Name, CustomerTypeID) VALUES
        (2, 'Ane Anderson', 'O');
```

We can specify the keyword NULL instead of ignoring the columns.

```sql
INSERT INTO dbo.Customer (CustomerID, Name, Address, Zipcode, CustomerTypeID) VALUES
        (3, 'Company1', NULL, NULL, 'C');
```

This is interesting if we use a table value constructor and insert several rows at the same time. Some Customers have an Address and a Zipcode, others do not.

```sql
INSERT INTO dbo.Customer (CustomerID, Name, Address, Zipcode, CustomerTypeID) VALUES
        (5, 'Peter Poulsen', NULL, NULL, 'O'),
        (6, 'Irene Knudsen', 'Torvet 13', 8000, 'O');
```

If we specify the column list, the columns can be specified in random order, just the column list and the value list are in the same order.

```
INSERT INTO dbo.Customer (Name, CustomerTypeID, Address, Zipcode, CustomerID) VALUES
        ('Company2', 'C', NULL, NULL, 4);
```

For the last INSERT example, we create a table with new customers. This table is named dbo.NewCust. The rows from this new table are then inserted into the dbo.Customer table. First we create the new table. By doing it in the following way, we are sure that all columns in dbo.Customer are also in the dbo.NewCust table. The corresponding columns have the same data type and nullability. The constraints are not added to the new table. We create the table and add two rows to the table. Using TOP 0 when creating the new table only the structure are created and no rows are copied into the table. Instead of TOP 0 we could have specified WHERE 1 = 0 which will also ignore all rows as the condition is always false.

```
SELECT   TOP 0
        CustomerID,
        Name,
        Address,
        Zipcode,
        CustomerTypeID
        INTO dbo.NewCust
        FROM dbo.Customer;
GO
INSERT INTO dbo.NewCust (CustomerID, Name, Address, Zipcode, CustomerTypeID) VALUES
        (101, 'Nick Nielsen', NULL, NULL, 'O'),      (102, 'Shop 199', 'Torvet 23', 9000, 'C');
```

We can then use INSERT statement combined with a SELECT statement to copy all rows from dbo.NewCust table to the dbo.Customer table. The keyword VALUES must not be specified. The column list can be exclude but never do this in production.

```
INSERT INTO dbo.Customer (CustomerID, Name, Address, Zipcode, CustomerTypeID)
        SELECT   CustomerID,
                Name,
                Address,
                Zipcode,
                CustomerTypeID
                FROM dbo.NewCust;
```

The SELECT statement can also contain a constant or refer to a function such as SYSDATETIME() if the receiving table has columns for this information. The constant can be used to indicate where the data comes from/is born. In the following example, all Employees are added as Customers. Of course, CustomerType 'E' must first be added to the dbo.CustomerType table.

```
INSERT INTO dbo.Customer (CustomerID, Name, Address, Zipcode, CustomerTypeID)
        SELECT   CustomerID,
                Name,
                Address,
                Zipcode,
                'E'
                FROM dbo.Employee;
```

UPDATE

With UPDATE we can change data in a table. In the first example we change the Address and Zipcode for one of the Customers added above.

```
UPDATE   dbo.Customer
        SET Address = 'Vestergade 45', Zipcode = 9000
        WHERE CustomerID = 6;
```

Because we reference the PRIMARY KEY CustomerID, we change zero or one row. It is not an error if zero rows are changed because the CustomerID does not exist. We can use @@ROWCOUNT to test if it is zero or one row.

```
SELECT @@ROWCOUNT;
```

If we want to update all rows we can update all rows in the table by excluding the WHERE clause from the statement. It is more problematic if we forget the WHERE clause. We can embed the UPDATE - or several UPDATE statements - in a transaction, and then execute COMMIT TRANSACTION if the expected happens or ROLLBACK TRANSACTION if we want to undo all changes since BEGIN TRANSACTION. Note that @@ROWCOUNT only returns the number of changed rows from the last executed statement, so if several UPDATE statements are executed, @@ROWCOUNT should perhaps be tested for each individual statement.

```
BEGIN TRANSACTION;

UPDATE dbo.Customer
        SET Address = 'Vestergade 45', Zipcode = 9000
        WHERE CustomerID = 6;

SELECT @@ROWCOUNT;

-- COMMIT TRANSACTION
-- ROLLBACK TRANSACTION;
```

A BEGIN TRANSACTION must always be followed later by COMMIT or ROLLBACK. By specifying these two statements as a comment, we don't suddenly perform COMMIT by a mistake. We cannot perform ROLLBACK on an already committed transaction.

If we have a table dbo.Product with a column with the Price of the Product, we can make a price increase on all products with the following statement. Since no WHERE clause is specified, the update applies to all rows. If we in the WHERE clause have a condition that reference the ProductID or refers to e.g. a ProductCategory, the changes will of course only be for these Products. Since the increase must be 5%, a calculation is made for each product in relation to the existing price. The expression in the WHERE clause can be any of the expressions that we will learn later when we look at the WHERE clause of the SELECT statement.

```
UPDATE    dbo.Product
        SET Price = Price * 1.05;
```

If we want to delete the address information for a Customer but keep the Customer row, we need to change the columns to NULL.

```
UPDATE    dbo.Customer
        SET Address = NULL, Zipcode = NULL
        WHERE CustomerID = 6;
```

It is possible to have all the desired changes in a table and then use a join to update the rows. We create a table dbo.UpdCust and use this table to update multiple customers. Think of this not as customers that can be updated immediately, but a table of changes to Product information's. We do not want to update Name and Price during the day, but only in a job that is executed at night, so the changes will be ready for the next day. The changes are entered during the day and stored in a table. In the example we use Customers because we have this table.

```
SELECT    TOP 0
        CustomerID,
        Name,
        Address,
        Zipcode
        INTO dbo.UpdCust
        FROM dbo.Customer;

INSERT INTO dbo.UpdCust (CustomerID, Name, Address, Zipcode) VALUES
        (2, 'Ane Marie Andersen', 'Nygade 3', 2000),          (6, 'Irene Carlsen', 'Vestergade 45', 9000);
GO
```

```
UPDATE   dbo.Customer
    SET       CustomerID = UpdCust.CustomerID,
              Name = UpdCust.Name,
              Address = UpdCust.Address,
              Zipcode = UpdCust.Zipcode
    FROM dbo.Customer INNER JOIN dbo.UpdCust ON Customer.CustomerID = UpdCust.CustomerID;
```

Remember again to use user-defined transactions when changing data.

DELETE

With DELETE we remove rows from a table. As shown above with UPDATE we can delete values in some of the columns in a row by updating the columns to NULL. But for removing the row DELETE is used.

DELETE removes all rows from a table if no WHERE clause is specified. The table still exists, but is empty. The following DELETE statement removes zero or one row depending on whether a Customer with CustomerID = 3 exists in the table. CustomerID is the PRIMARY KEY, so only delete of zero or one row. We always wrap the statement in a user-defined transaction, as described above, and evaluate the global variable @@ROWCOUNT.

```
DELETE
    FROM dbo.Customer
    WHERE CustomerID = 3;
```

We can also delete rows depending on values in another table.

```
SELECT   TOP 0
         CustomerID
         INTO dbo.DelCust
         FROM dbo.Customer;

INSERT INTO dbo.DelCust (CustomerID) VALUES
         (2),      (6);
```

The first FROM in the following statement is the table from which the rows are deleted. The second FROM is used for the condition. In this example, the condition is that the same CustomerID value exists in dbo.DelCust table and in dbo.Customer. If we have a CustomerID value in dbo.DelCust that does not exist in dbo.Customer, the Join condition is false, so no rows are deleted. This is not an error, as it is allowed to delete 0 rows.

```
DELETE
    FROM dbo.Customer
    FROM dbo.Customer INNER JOIN dbo.DelCust ON Customer.CustomerID = DelCust.CustomerID;
```

The above DELETE can also be written in one of the following ways, where we use IN and EXISTS.

```DELETE FROM dbo.Customer WHERE CustomerID IN (SELECT CustomerID FROM bo.DelCust);```	```DELETE FROM dbo.Customer WHERE EXISTS (SELECT * FROM dbo.DelCust WHERE Customer.CustomerID = delCust.CustomerID);```

TRUNCATE

The TRUNCATE statement also deletes rows in a table. Unfortunately, there are many myths about TRUNCATE, so we try to dispel these. TRUNCATE is used when the table is emptied. If the table is partitioned we can use TRUNCATE to only empty some of the partitions.

TRUNCATE cannot be rolled back with the statement ROLLBACK TRANSACTION. This is not correct in SQL Server. The problem may arise because the statement is just executed as

```
TRUNCATE
        TABLE dbo.Customer;
```

If we do not specify a user-defined transaction, the statement is wrapped in an implicit transaction. So the following is executed

```
BEGIN TRANSACTION;

TRUNCATE
        TABLE dbo.Customer;

COMMIT TRANSACTION;
```

As described earlier in the chapter, it is not possible to perform a ROLLBACK if the COMMIT has already been performed. Therefore, the problem is not how TRUNCATE is executed, but that the statement is not executed in a user-defined transaction. The same principles apply as for INSERT, UPDATE and DELETE.

SQL Server does not store data in the log about rows that are removed, but only information about the pages where the rows were stored. A page is a 8KB block When the transaction is complete, a background process is executed to release these pages for reuse. If we perform a ROLLBACK, this operation is not performed, and therefore the table still contains all the rows.

Try to think about what will happen if SQL Server crashes in the middle of performing a TRUNCATE operation on a very large table. What has been deleted and what needs to be deleted? After a crash, it should be possible for SQL Server to restart without user interaction. But even worse. In SQL Server, it is possible only deleting some of the rows in a table with TRUNCATE if the table is partitioned.

```
CREATE DATABASE PartitionDB
ON PRIMARY
        (NAME = PartitionDB_sys,
        FILENAME = 'c:\Databases\PartitionDB_sys.mdf',
        SIZE = 5MB),

FILEGROUP PartitionDB_fg1
        (NAME = PartitionDB_fg1,
        FILENAME = 'c:\Databases\PartitionDB_fg1.ndf',
        SIZE = 200MB),
FILEGROUP PartitionDB_fg2
        (NAME = PartitionDB_fg2,
        FILENAME = 'c:\Databases\PartitionDB_fg2.ndf',
        SIZE = 200MB),
FILEGROUP PartitionDB_fg3
        (NAME = PartitionDB_fg3,
        FILENAME = 'c:\Databases\PartitionDB_fg3.ndf',
        SIZE = 200MB)
LOG ON
        (NAME = PartitionDB_log,
        FILENAME = 'c:\Databases\PartitionDB.ldf',
        SIZE = 400MB);
GO
```

With the following definition we have a table dbo.PartitionTable where the borders between the three partitions are defined with the PARTITION FUNCTION and the PARTITION SCHEME statement.

```
USE PartitionDB

CREATE PARTITION FUNCTION PartitionFunction (DATE)
        AS RANGE RIGHT FOR VALUES ('2024-2-1', '2024-3-1');
GO
CREATE PARTITION SCHEME PartitionScheme
        AS PARTITION PartitionFunction TO (PartitionDB_fg1, PartitionDB_fg2, PartitionDB_fg3);
GO
```

```
CREATE TABLE dbo.PartitionTable
(
        ID                   INT      NOT NULL          IDENTITY,
...
        TransactionTime      DATE     NOT NULL,
        MonthNo              AS       MONTH (TransactionTime) PERSISTED,

        CONSTRAINT PK_PartitionTable PRIMARY KEY (ID, TransactionTime)
) ON PartitionScheme (TransactionTime);
```

We can of course execute INSERT, UPDATE and DELETE statements to manipulate one or more rows. If we INSERT a row with TransactionTime = '2024-2-15' the data is stored in PartitionDB_fg2. If TransactionTime is '2024-1-12' the data is stored in PartitionDB_fg1, etc. If we want to remove all rows in the table we can execute

```
TRUNCATE TABLE dbo.PartitionTable;
```

However, if we only want to remove some of the rows, we can use TRUNCATE and specifying one or some of the partitions. In the following example, all the rows from Partition 1 are still in the table after performing TRUNCATE. This can be used in a Data Warehouse, where we each month add a new Partition for the upcoming month, but also empty the oldest month. By using TRUNCATE instead of DELETE, we have a faster operation with less data stored in the log file.

```
TRUNCATE TABLE dbo.PartitionTable
        WITH (PARTITIONS (2, 3));
```

If we have an IDENTITY column and TRUNCATE is performed, the next value is reset to the starting number from the definition of IDENTITY. If we use TRUNCATE and specify partitions, we continue from the value we reached before we performed TRUNCATE.

In this example, only Partition 2 and 3 are emptied, but rows from Partition 1 are still in the table. Many think that it is very important to point out that TRUNCATE is a DDL/Definition statement and not a DML/Manipulation statement. My understanding of categorization of statements in SQL says that TRUNCATE is a DML. A previous incorrect categorization is obviously hard to kill. We are manipulating data in the table and even only some of the data. The table definition is kept unchanged. Categorisations should aid understanding and not cause ambiguity! Many point out that only all rows can be deleted with TRUNCATE. This may be true for some database systems, but not for SQL Server. So more DML than DDL!

MERGE

This chapter provides a general overview of the MERGE statement. The purpose is to understand the statement if a system is to be maintained and not to provide knowledge to be able to develop or maintain advanced versions of the statement.

With MERGE we work with two tables - target and source. The target table needs to be modified with the data that appears in the source table. Some rows need to be inserted and other rows need to be either updated or deleted. MERGE is used because all types of operations can be specified in one statement. The construction has many similarities to a CASE.

We use the dbo.Customer table created above and INSERT the rows we want for the example. We use the following data for showing what happens. We are also creating the table dbo.ChangeCust using a row constructer known from INSERT. The row constructer is used just for showing and learning how a table can be created when evaluating.

```
INSERT INTO dbo.Customer (CustomerID, Name, Address, Zipcode, CustomerTypeID) VALUES
        (1, 'John Olsson', 'Nygade 22', 2000, 'O'),      (2, 'Ane Anderson', 'Strandvejen 144', 5000, 'O'),
        (3, 'Company1', 'Nygade 51', 8000, 'C'),         (5, 'Peter Poulsen', NULL, NULL, 'O'),
        (6, 'Irene Knudsen', 'Torvet 13', 8000, 'O');
```

```
SELECT    *
          INTO dbo.ChangeCust
          FROM (VALUES    (3, 'Company aps', 'Bygaden 3', 9000, 'C'),    (7, 'Peter Chris', 'Nygade 34', 5000, 'O'),
                          (8, 'Ivan Larsen', 'Havnen 2', 5000, 'O'))    AS Cust (CustomerID, Name, Address, Zipcode, CustomerTypeID);
```

The following statement MERGEs data from the two tables. We use the expression specified under TO for each row in dbo.ChangeCust compared to the rows in dbo.Customer to choose one of the following operations.

- WHEN MATCHED – when the expression in ON returns true we have the same value in CustomerID and a row in dbo.Customer must be updated.
- WHEN NOT MATCHED – when we have an expression in ON that returns false we add a new row to the dbo.Customer table.

We never specify a table after the INSERT, UPDATE or DELETE statements because it is already specified as the target table after the keyword MERGE. In the example it is dbo.Customer.

```
MERGE     dbo.Customer
          USING dbo.ChangeCust
          ON Customer.CustomerID = ChangeCust.CustomerID
          WHEN MATCHED        THEN      UPDATE SET        Customer.Name = ChangeCust.Name,
                                                          Customer.Address = ChangeCust.Address,
                                                          Customer.Zipcode = ChangeCust.Zipcode
          WHEN NOT MATCHED THEN       INSERT VALUES (ChangeCust.CustomerID, ChangeCust.Name, ChangeCust.Address,
                                                          ChangeCust.Zipcode, ChangeCust.CustomerTypeID)
          OUTPUT DELETED.*, INSERTED.*;
```

Using of the OUTPUT clause is optional. We return the data corresponding to the data written to the Log. The table DELETED contains data corresponding to BeforeImage and INSERTED is the data corresponding to the AfterImage. After performing the operation, the following data is returned from OUTPUT. We can see that CustomerID = 3 is Updated because we have both DELETED and INSERTED data. CustomerID 7 and 8 are new because we only have INSERTED data.

DELETED					INSERTED				
CustomerID	Name	Address	Zipcode	CustomerTypeID	CustomerID	Name	Address	Zipcode	CustomerTypeID
3	Company1	Nygade 51	8000	C	3	Company aps	Bygaden 3	9000	C
NULL	NULL	NULL	NULL	NULL	7	Peter Chris	Nygade 34	5000	O
NULL	NULL	NULL	NULL	NULL	8	Ivan Larsen	Havnen 2	5000	O

To evaluate the statement, we can use the following data. Instead of using a table as the source/USING, we use a row constructor in the MERGE statement. Of course, we cannot use a row constructor for the target table because we must have a table where the result is stored. If we specify a user-defined transaction, we can ROLLBACK all the changes and try again with the same or modified data.

In the example we add a column in the transaction data specifying whether a CustomerID should be deleted. Do not use a row constructor in production only when evaluating.

```
MERGE     dbo.Customer
          USING (VALUES    (3, 'Company aps', 'Bygaden 3', 9000, 'C', NULL),    (7, 'Peter Christoffersen', 'Nygade 34', 5000, 'O', NULL),
                           (8, 'Ivan Larsen', 'Havnen 2', 5000, 'O', NULL),    (5, NULL, NULL, NULL, NULL, 'Del'))
                           AS ChangeCust (CustomerID, Name, Address, Zipcode, CustomerTypeID, DelCust)
          ON Customer.CustomerID = ChangeCust.CustomerID
          WHEN      MATCHED           AND
                    ChangeCust.DelCust = 'Del'        THEN DELETE
          WHEN      MATCHED                           THEN UPDATE SET      Customer.Name = ChangeCust.Name,
                                                                          Customer.Address = ChangeCust.Address,
                                                                          Customer.Zipcode = ChangeCust.Zipcode
          WHEN      NOT MATCHED                       THEN INSERT VALUES (ChangeCust.CustomerID, ChangeCust.Name, ChangeCust.Address,
                                                                          ChangeCust.Zipcode, ChangeCust.CustomerTypeID)
          OUTPUT DELETED.*, INSERTED.*;
```

In the statement we have two MATCHED blocks. The statement evaluate WHEN in the same way as in a CASE. It is therefore important that the DELETE-MATCHED comes first. Else the data is updated in UPDATE-

MATCHED and the DELETE-MATCHED will never be evaluated. CustomerID is deleted because we have deleted data and not inserted data.

The result returned from OUTPUT is.

DELETED					INSERTED				
CustomerID	Name	Address	Zipcode	Customer-TypeID	CustomerID	Name	Address	Zipcode	Customer-TypeID
3	Company1	Nygade 51	8000	C	3	Company aps	Bygaden 3	9000	C
NULL	NULL	NULL	NULL	NULL	7	Peter Christoffersen	Nygade 34	5000	O
NULL	NULL	NULL	NULL	NULL	8	Ivan Larsen	Havnen 2	5000	O
5	Peter Poulsen	NULL	NULL	O	NULL	NULL	NULL	NULL	NULL

SELECT

With SELECT data is read from one or more tables. The statement consists of 6 points. When writing a SELECT statement, the order as indicated below must be observed, but it is not necessary that all 6 clauses are included. It is also important to emphasize that the order in which the individual parts are written does not reflect the order in which they are executed. SQL is based on mathematics and when talking about manipulation, a distinction is made between

- Algebra language or procedural language, where it is specified how to arrive at a result. This is typically true for the various programming languages such as C# and Java.
- Calculus languages or non-procedural/declarative languages are those languages where the final result is specified. But how to get to the result is not an issue. The same statement can be executed differently depending on search conditions, defined indexes, …. The database system is responsible for finding the best way to get to the result.

Since SQL is basically a declarative language, you should focus on specifying the correct result and not make too much thought about how the database system will find the correct result. Since the same result in some situations can be expressed in several ways, you must of course choose the statement having the best performance.

Avoid making HOW solutions, e.g. by storing intermediate results in temporary tables. As a general recommendation, this will result in worse execution time than writing a one-statement solution. It is important to try the different solutions, but always try to solve the problem by writing only one statement. Try spending some time to see if another way of describing the solution will give the same result. It can be a good way to see perhaps not so good solution proposals. If a solution uses temporary tables then try to build it all together into a statement using CTE.

The SELECT statement consists of the following 6 clauses

```
SELECT   Projection
         FROM Tables
         WHERE Selection condition
         GROUP BY Grouping columns
         HAVING Grouping condition
         ORDER BY Sort columns
```

When SQL was developed, it was decided that this was the order the statement should be written in. They could just as easily have chosen a different order. But that doesn't matter since it's a declarative statement.

In the following, the 6 clauses are reviewed.

Projection

The result from performing a SELECT statement is always a table. In the Projection, the structure of the result table is specified. It is important that as few columns as possible is returned from the execution. Fewer column will give a better performance. The following shows the possibilities. The options can be combined.

Declaration	Meaning
*	All columns from the tables listed under FROM are included in the results table.
Tabel.*	If more than one table is specified in FROM, table.* will include all the columns from the specified table
Column2, Column3	A comma-separated list of the columns to be included in the results. A column name can be specified, but specify table.column in production systems. It will be more maintenance-friendly to read the statement if it is clear from which table the column is retrieved. If two or more of the tables specified in the FROM clause have columns with the same name, table.column must be used.
Function	Functions can be used. There are function for 'calculating' the first letter of a Name and to calculate the parts that make up a date. It could be the function that return today date. Later in the book there is a chapter about the most used system functions. The Function can also be an user defined Function.
Calculation/expressions	A calculation expression can be written.
Constant	If we want a value in each result row we can specify a constant.

TOP x TOP x PERCENT	With TOP, it is possible to limit the number of rows in the results table. x indicates the number. If TOP is specified without specifying ORDER BY, it is random rows that is returned. If ORDER BY is specified, it is x number of rows based on the sort order.
DISTINCT	DISTINCT indicates that there must not be duplicated rows in the result table. Although DISTINCT is specified right after the keyword SELECT, it applies to the entire row in the result table.
Alias Name	If a column is the result of a calculation the column does not have a name. The column is giving a name by specifying an alias name. If a columns name is bad we can change it in the result table by specifying an alias name. An alias name is only used for the result table and has no influence on metadata for the table

In the following we are looking at some examples. We use the following tables.

```sql
CREATE TABLE dbo.Zipinfo
(
        Zipcode            SMALLINT        NOT NULL
                           CONSTRAINT PK_Zipinfo PRIMARY KEY,
        City               VARCHAR (20)    NOT NULL
);

CREATE TABLE dbo.Customer
(
        CustomerID         INT             NOT NULL
                           CONSTRAINT PK_Customer PRIMARY KEY,
        Name               VARCHAR (35)    NOT NULL,
        Address            VARCHAR (35)    NULL,
        Zipcode            SMALLINT        NULL
                           CONSTRAINT FK_Customer_Zipinfo FOREIGN KEY REFERENCES dbo.Zipinfo (Zipcode)
);
GO
INSERT INTO dbo.Zipinfo (Zipcode, City) VALUES
        (5000, 'Odense'),          (6000, 'Kolding'),          (8000, 'Aarhus C'),          (9000, 'Aalborg');

INSERT INTO dbo.Customer (CustomerID, Name, Address, Zipcode) VALUES
        (23, 'Peter Poulsen', NULL, NULL),          (47, 'Irene Knudsen', 'Vestergade 13', 8000),
        (11, 'Claus Jensen', 'Torvet 13', 6000),    (16, 'Per Larsen', 'Storegade 45', 9000),
        (78, 'Ida Thomsen', 'Lilletorv 17', 5000),  (99, 'Hans Knudsen', 'Torvet 2', 5000),
        (13, 'Jens Andersen', 'Havnegade 27', 9000),(65, 'Ane Olsen', 'Vestergade 47', 8000),
        (71, 'Maren Kristensen', 'Strandvejen 111', 8000);
```

In the first example, we look at using * in the Projection. The results table will include all the columns that are in the tables listed under FROM.

When developing a statement, it may be useful to start by specifying *. Start by figuring out which tables are to be included in the statement, how these tables are to be joined, and what selection conditions apply. It is possible to evaluate the statement continuously. There are no columns specified in the projection that cannot be found in any table in FROM. If four tables are to be joined and three selection conditions must also be met, two of the tables can be joined and the result evaluated. Then the third table can be added and the result tested. Then we can add the first selection condition and the statement can be evaluated, etc. etc. In this way, it is easier to understand the statement that is being developed and to find any errors.

Only when the 'correct' result is found do we change * to the desired columns. There are performance benefits to specifying only the columns that are to be used. If a table has 20 columns and only 15 are to be used, these 15 should be specified. It takes time to build the result table, so fewer columns leads to better performance. It is an advantage to make it a habit to start with *, but always remember to switch to a column list when we have found the desired data for the task.

By limiting the number of columns, data may be read from a covered index instead of from the table. This can improve performance. Less data is also sent over the network, which can be an advantage for large amounts of data.

The following example shows the use of *.

```sql
SELECT      *
        FROM dbo.Customer;
```

CustomerID	Name	Address	Zipcode
11	Claus Jensen	Torvet 13	6000
13	Jens Andersen	Havnegade 27	9000
16	Per Larsen	Storegade 45	9000
23	Peter Poulsen	NULL	NULL
47	Irene Knudsen	Vestergade 13	8000
65	Ane Olsen	Vestergade 47	8000
71	Maren Kristensen	Strandvejen 111	8000
78	Ida Thomsen	Lilletorv 17	5000
99	Hans Knudsen	Torvet 2	5000

In the next example there are 2 tables in the FROM clause. The table dbo.Customer has 4 columns and the table dbo. Zipinfo has 2 columns. Since * is entered, there will be 6 columns in the results table. There are 2 columns with the column name Zipcode. This can cause problems when using the data.

```
SELECT      *
            FROM dbo.Customer INNER JOIN dbo.Zipinfo ON Customer.Zipcode = Zipinfo.Zipcode;
```

CustomerID	Name	Address	Zipcode	Zipcode	City
11	Claus Jensen	Torvet 13	6000	6000	Kolding
13	Jens Andersen	Havnegade 27	9000	9000	Aalborg
16	Per Larsen	Storegade 45	9000	9000	Aalborg
47	Irene Knudsen	Vestergade 13	8000	8000	Aarhus C
65	Ane Olsen	Vestergade 47	8000	8000	Aarhus C
71	Maren Kristensen	Strandvejen 111	8000	8000	Aarhus C
78	Ida Thomsen	Lilletorv 17	5000	5000	Odense
99	Hans Knudsen	Torvet 2	5000	5000	Odense

This problem has subsequently been solved. In the first statement, all columns from dbo.Customer table are included and only the City column from dbo.Zipinfo. The second statement includes the CustomerID, Name and Address columns from dbo.Customer and all columns from dbo.Zipinfo.

```
SELECT      Customer.*,
            Zipinfo.City
            FROM dbo.Customer INNER JOIN dbo.Zipinfo ON Customer.Zipcode = Zipinfo.Zipcode;

SELECT      Customer.CustomerID,
            Customer.Name,
            Customer.Address,
            Zipinfo.*
            FROM dbo.Customer INNER JOIN dbo.Zipinfo ON Customer.Zipcode = Zipinfo.Zipcode;
```

For both statements we have the following result.

CustomerID	Name	Address	Zipcode	City
11	Claus Jensen	Torvet 13	6000	Kolding
13	Jens Andersen	Havnegade 27	9000	Aalborg
16	Per Larsen	Storegade 45	9000	Aalborg
47	Irene Knudsen	Vestergade 13	8000	Aarhus C
65	Ane Olsen	Vestergade 47	8000	Aarhus C
71	Maren Kristensen	Strandvejen 111	8000	Aarhus C
78	Ida Thomsen	Lilletorv 17	5000	Odense
99	Hans Knudsen	Torvet 2	5000	Odense

The next statement shows that what we specify in the projection is included in the result table. It is not evaluated for reasonableness. The statement refers to the dbo.Zipinfo table in FROM. This table has 2 columns, but * is specified 3 times along with the City column twice. The result table will contain 8 columns.

```
SELECT      *, *, *,
            City, City
            FROM dbo.Zipinfo;
```

Zipcode	City	Zipcode	City	Zipcode	City	City	City
5000	Odense	5000	Odense	5000	Odense	Odense	Odense
6000	Kolding	6000	Kolding	6000	Kolding	Kolding	Kolding
8000	Aarhus C	8000	Aarhus C	8000	Aarhus C	Aarhus C	Aarhus C
9000	Aalborg	9000	Aalborg	9000	Aalborg	Aalborg	Aalborg

When specifying expressions in Projections, the columns data types must be taken into account. Numerical data types can be added, multiplied etc. String data types can be concatenated, and on the date and time data types, direct calculations cannot be made, but date and time functions be used.

In the first example we want to concatenate Zipcode and City. Because the column Zipcode is numeric and City is alphanumeric we can do it in two ways. If we use the function CONCAT all columns specified as a parameter to the function which not have one of the string data type is automatically converted to a string. This is shown for Address1 below.

If we use the concatenation operator '+' we must convert non string columns to a column with one of the string data types using CAST before concatenating the values. Because Zipcode has the data type SMALLINT the value are converted to a VARCHAR (6). SMALLINT accepts values from -32768 to 32767. The data type is used when deciding what to do and not the knowledge of legal Zipcode values.

```
SELECT    Name,
          Address,
          CONCAT (Zipinfo.Zipcode, ' ', Zipinfo.City)               AS Address1,
          CAST (Zipinfo.Zipcode AS VARCHAR (6)) + ' ' + Zipinfo.City    AS Address2,
          Customer.Zipcode / 1000                                   AS Region
          FROM dbo.Customer INNER JOIN dbo.Zipinfo ON Customer.Zipcode = Zipinfo.Zipcode;
```

The column Region in the result is a division of the Zipcode value by 1000. When we are calculating on integer values the result is an integer. 9000 / 1000 is 9. But 9999 / 1000 also gives the result 9. If the column is defined as a string, the function LEFT is used instead.

As can be seen from the overview below, it can be difficult to get an overview of all the options. If the data type is not taken into account, maybe the statement does not fail today, but maybe later.

Expression	Result	Comment
9999 / 1000	9	When dividing integers, the result is an integer. No rounding is done, decimals are truncated.
'9990' / 1000	9	The expression is numerical, since division is a numerical operator. Therefore, an implicit conversion of the string to a number occurs. Since the string '9999' can be converted to a number, there will be no errors.
LEFT (9999, 1)	9	LEFT is a string function. The numeric value 9999 is implicit converted to a string. The string will be '9999' and the first character of the string is 9.
0800 / 1000	0	The expression is an integer division. No errors. The result is truncated to an integer, so the result is 0
'0800' / 1000	0	The string can be converted to the numeric value 800. The result is 0.
LEFT (0800, 1)	8	Leading zeros in a numeric value are ignored, the value will be converted to the string '800'. LEFT of this string is 8. If the numeric value is entered as 000000800 the result will still be 8 as the 6 leading zeros are ignored.
LEFT ('0800', 1)	0	The first character is 0. Since LEFT is a string function. 0 is returned.

When using TOP, it is important to focus on whether ORDER BY is also specified. If we specify TOP without ORDER BY, it is random which rows are returned. It depends on the generated execution plan. TOP 5 will be the first 5 rows read. If ORDER BY is specified, these are the top rows in relation to the sort order. It is allowed to ORDER BY a column that is not a column in the result table.

SELECT TOP 5	SELECT TOP 5	SELECT TOP 5
Name,	Name,	Name,
Address	Address	Address
FROM dbo.Customer;	FROM dbo.Customer	FROM dbo.Customer
	ORDER BY Name;	ORDER BY Zipcode;

Name	Address	Name	Address	Name	Address
Claus Jensen	Torvet 13	Ane Olsen	Vestergade 47	Peter Poulsen	NULL
Jens Andersen	Havnegade 27	Claus Jensen	Torvet 13	Ida Thomsen	Lilletorv 17
Per Larsen	Storegade 45	Hans Knudsen	Torvet 2	Hans Knudsen	Torvet 2
Peter Poulsen	NULL	Ida Thomsen	Lilletorv 17	Claus Jensen	Torvet 13
Irene Knudsen	Vestergade 13	Irene Knudsen	Vestergade 13	Ane Olsen	Vestergade 47

In the statement above, we use alias names for the calculated columns. It is not only for calculated columns alias name can be specified, but can also be used for a column because the column name is 'bad' or because the result table is used directly in a tool such as Excel and we want a better/more descriptive name.

With DISTINCT we only have unique rows in the result table. DISTINCT is specified first after SELECT, but it is the result rows that is DISTINCT. It is important that DISTINCT does not guarantee the sorting order. If the result is to be sorted, ORDER BY must also be specified.

For statement number 2 below DISTINCT should not be specified because the tables PRIMARY KEY is a column in the result table and the table only have unique values for this column.

```
SELECT  DISTINCT              SELECT  DISTINCT              SELECT  DISTINCT
        Zipcode                       CustomerID,                   CustomerID,
        FROM dbo.Customer;            Zipcode                       Zipcode
                                      FROM dbo.Customer;            FROM dbo.Customer
                                                                    ORDER BY Zipcode;
```

Zipcode
NULL
5000
6000
8000
9000

CustomerID	Zipcode
11	6000
13	9000
16	9000
23	NULL
47	8000
65	8000
71	8000
78	5000
99	5000

CustomerID	Zipcode
23	NULL
78	5000
99	5000
11	6000
47	8000
65	8000
71	8000
13	9000
16	9000

FROM

In the FROM clause, one or multiple tables can be specified. When designing a database, we split data into multiple tables to avoid redundancy. It is therefore necessary to combine the information from several tables into one result table when querying the database. The operation to combine data from multiple tables is Join. It is important to know that join is a binary operation. We can join two tables, which results in a table as an intermediate result. To this intermediate result we can join a third table, which gives a new table as an intermediate result. To this intermediate result we can join the fourth table, etc. This is exactly the same as performing calculations on numerical values. If we look at the following numerical calculation.

$$14 + 5 + 16 + 15$$

we add 14 and 5 which gives the result 19. The expression is now reduced to

$$19 + 16 + 15$$

Then we add 19 and 16 giving 35. The expression is now

$$35 + 15$$

We end up with the result 50 after adding 35 and 15.

If we look more at the numerical values, we may see that it will be more 'optimal' by first adding 14 and 16 and then 5 and 15. For the result of the expression we then add 30 and 20.

Similarly, SQL Server's compiler/optimizer may choose not joining multiple tables in the order we specify. We should not make too much effort about this, as a change in order will produce the result that we have specified. In previous versions of SQL Server this could be a problem, but now the vast majority of queries will benefit from it. If we join multiple tables, the precedence rule is that they are logically joined from left to right.

We use the following four tables which are similar to the tables we have seen used before. Note that the customers have CustomerID values 1, 2, 3, 4, ... A little trick, as it will then be easier to verify which customers are included in the result table. Do not use large production tables in the beginning when learning! Use realistic data as they are easier to understand. In the example the Zipcodes exists and GenderCode is realistic.

```
CREATE TABLE dbo.Zipinfo
(
        Zipcode    SMALLINT              NOT NULL
                   CONSTRAINT PK_Zipinfo PRIMARY KEY,
        City       VARCHAR (20)          NOT NULL
);
```

```
CREATE TABLE dbo.Customertype
(
        CustomertypeID    SMALLINT            NOT NULL
                          CONSTRAINT PK_Customertype
                          PRIMARY KEY,
        CustomertypeTxt   VARCHAR (20)        NOT NULL
);
```

```
INSERT INTO dbo.Zipinfo (Zipcode, City) VALUES
        (2000, 'Frederiksberg'),    (4000, 'Roskilde'),
        (5000, 'Odense'),           (6000, 'Kolding'),
        (8000, 'Aarhus C'),         (9000, 'Aalborg');
```

```
INSERT INTO dbo.Gender (Gendercode, GenderTxt) VALUES
        ('F', 'Female'),         ('M', 'Male');
```

```
CREATE TABLE dbo.Gender
(
        Gendercode        CHAR (1)        NOT NULL
                          CONSTRAINT PK_Gender PRIMARY KEY,
        GenderTxt         VARCHAR (10)    NOT NULL
);
```

```
INSERT INTO dbo.Customertype (CustomertypeID, CustomertypeTxt) VALUES
        (1, 'Private'),       (2, 'Company'),      (3, 'Public')
```

We now have all the code tables and can create the dbo.Customer table.

```
CREATE TABLE dbo.Customer
(
        CustomerID        INT             NOT NULL
                          CONSTRAINT PK_Customer PRIMARY KEY,
        Name              VARCHAR (35)    NOT NULL,
        Address           VARCHAR (35)    NULL,
        Zipcode           SMALLINT        NULL
                          CONSTRAINT FK_Customer_Zipinfo FOREIGN KEY REFERENCES dbo.Zipinfo (Zipcode),
        Gendercode        CHAR (1)        NULL
                          CONSTRAINT FK_Customer_Gender FOREIGN KEY REFERENCES dbo.Gender (Gendercode),
        CustomertypeID    SMALLINT        NOT NULL
                          CONSTRAINT FK_Customer_Customertype FOREIGN KEY REFERENCES dbo.Customertype (CustomertypeID)
);
GO
INSERT INTO dbo.Customer (CustomerID, Name, Address, Zipcode, Gendercode, CustomertypeID) VALUES
        (1, 'Peter Poulsen', NULL, NULL, NULL, 1),        (2, 'Irene Knudsen', 'Vestergade 13', 8000, 'F', 1),
        (3, 'Claus Jensen', 'Torvet 13', 6000, 'M', 1),   (4, 'Per Larsen', 'Storegade 45', 9000, 'M', 1),
        (5, 'Hairdresser Tina', 'Lilletorv 17', 5000, NULL, 2),  (6, 'Newsstand', 'Torvet 2', 5000, NULL, 2),
        (7, 'Jens Andersen', 'Havnegade 27', 9000, NULL, 1),     (8, 'Ane Olsen', 'Vestergade 47', 8000, 'F', 1),
        (9, 'Maren Kristensen', 'Strandvejen 111', 8000, 'F', 1);
```

There are several types of joins. We will look at all the different types, but start with the most commonly used – INNER JOIN. Just as important as choosing the right join type for the task, it is important to know the Join condition. And remember that the different join types are different operations and cannot simply be interchanged, but the correct one for the task must be chosen.

INNER JOIN

When we join two tables, we look at the first row in the first table and compare this to the first row in the second table. If the join condition evaluates to true, a row is inserted into the result table consisting of the columns/values from the two rows. Then, the join condition is evaluated by looking at the first row from the first table and the second row of the second table. If the join condition is true, a result row is created. If the condition is false, we continue to the next evaluation. Then the join condition between the first row from the first table and the third row from the second table is evaluated, and so on.

It's a bit of a complicated explanation, but is included to show that it's not a matter of the same value occurring in the two tables, but only whether the join condition evaluates to true or false.

In the following sketches, green lines is evaluation to TRUE and red lines is evaluation to FALSE when the join condition is evaluated comparing two rows.

We are looking at INNER JOIN. The Equi version is where the expression contains the comparison operator equal to/=. If the comparison operator is <, >, <>, ... it is called a Theta Join.

The Join Types in the following sketches are INNER JOIN because a row is added to the result table when the join condition evaluates to TRUE. We use the two table t1 and t2.

t1		t2		Result				Comment
								SELECT *
f1	**f2**	**f3**	**f4**	**f1**	**f2**	**f3**	**f4**	FROM t1 INNER JOIN t2 ON t1.f2 = t2.f4;
1	A	10	A	1	A	10	A	
2	A	11	B					A simple equi join where the values must be equal.
3	B	12	B					
4	F	13	C					When we evaluate the first row from t1 against the rows
								from t2 we have only one green line/one true.
f1	**f2**	**f3**	**f4**	**f1**	**f2**	**f3**	**f4**	
1	A	10	A	1	A	10	A	A = A, A = B, A = B, A = C
2	A	11	B	2	A	10	A	
3	B	12	B					One row is added to the result.
4	F	13	C					
								When we evaluate the second row from t1 with the rows
f1	**f2**	**f3**	**f4**	**f1**	**f2**	**f3**	**f4**	from t2 only one green line/one true.
1	A	10	A	1	A	10	A	
2	A	11	B	2	A	10	A	A = A, A = B, A = B, A = C
3	B	12	B	3	B	11	B	
4	F	13	C	3	B	12	B	One more row is added to the result.
f1	**f2**	**f3**	**f4**	**f1**	**f2**	**f3**	**f4**	When we evaluate the third row from t1 against the rows
1	A	10	A	1	A	10	A	from t2 we have two green lines/two true.
2	A	11	B	2	A	10	A	
3	B	12	B	3	B	11	B	B = A, B = B, B = B, B = C
4	F	13	C	3	B	12	B	
								We add two more rows to the result.
								When we evaluate the forth row from t1 with the rows from t2 we only have red lines. Therefore now rows are added to the result
								F = A, F = B, F = B, F = C
								The result table contains for this join four rows.

The next example is still an INNER JOIN and also an INNER EQUI JOIN. The join condition is a little bit special because it is a nonsense expression which is always true. It is an Equi Join because the comparison operator is '='.

t1		t2		Result				Comment
								SELECT *
f1	**f2**	**f3**	**f4**	**f1**	**f2**	**f3**	**f4**	FROM t1 INNER JOIN t2 ON 1 = 1;
1	A	10	A	1	A	10	A	
2	A	11	B	1	A	11	B	It is an Inner Equi Join where the values in the join
3	B	12	B	1	A	12	B	condition must be equal.
		13	C	1	A	13	C	
								But because 1 = 1 is always true all rows from t1 are
f1	**f2**	**f3**	**f4**	**f1**	**f2**	**f3**	**f4**	combined with all rows from t2.
1	A	10	A	1	A	10	A	
2	A	11	B	1	A	11	B	When we compare the first row from t1 with the four
3	B	12	B	1	A	12	B	rows from t2, the conditions are
		13	C	1	A	13	C	
				2	A	10	A	1 = 1, 1 = 1, 1 = 1 1 = 1.
				2	A	11	B	
				2	A	12	B	
				2	A	13	C	

f1	f2		f3	f4		f1	f2	f3	f4	All four conditions evaluates to true. We add four rows to the result.
1	A		10	A		1	A	10	A	
2	A		11	B		1	A	11	B	The same picture for the second and third row from t1.
3	B		12	B		1	A	12	B	
			13	C		1	A	13	C	The result contains 12 rows.
						2	A	10	A	
						2	A	11	B	
						2	A	12	B	
						2	A	13	C	
						3	B	10	A	
						3	B	11	B	
						3	B	12	B	
						3	B	13	C	

The following sketch is an INNER THETA JOIN. The join condition use '>' as comparison operator.

$$t1.f2 > t2.f4$$

t1	t2	Result	Comment
f1 f2: 1 A, 2 A, 3 B	f3 f4: 10 A, 11 B, 12 B, 13 C	f1 f2 f3 f4 (empty)	SELECT * FROM t1 INNER JOIN t2 ON t1.t2 > t2.f4; An Inner Theta Join. The four join conditions are A > A, A > B, A > B, A > C.
f1 f2: 1 A, 2 A, 3 B	f3 f4: 10 A, 11 B, 12 B, 13 C	f1 f2 f3 f4 (empty)	All evaluations are false. No rows are added to the result. For the second row from t1 we have the same conditions. A > A, A > B, A > B, A > C.
f1 f2: 1 A, 2 A, 3 B	f3 f4: 10 A, 11 B, 12 B, 13 C	f1 f2 f3 f4: 1 A 10 A	Still no rows are added to the result. When we compare the third row from t1 with the rows from t2 we have the following condition. B > A, B > B, B > B, B > C. The first condition is true. One row is added to the result

Hope these sketches show how the INNER JOIN operator works logically. SQL Server can generate an execution plan that works faster. In the above example, we have 12 comparisons. The optimizer can use an index if we have many rows and therefore only compare with some of the rows from the second table. But this is a task for the optimizer, we just write the join operation type and the desired join condition.

If we want to join three of the tables defined above we can develop the following statement.

The tables are dbo.Customer, dbo.Zipinfo and dbo.Customertype. In the example we have the same column name for the columns we use in the join condition. But the columns could have different names. We start writing

SELECT *

and wait changing * to the wanted Projection columns until we have joined the tables and maybe added a selection condition in WHERE clause. First we join the tables dbo.Customer and dbo.Zipinfo and specify the join condition after ON.

SELECT *
FROM dbo.Customer INNER JOIN dbo.Zipinfo ON Customer.Zipcode = Zipinfo.Zipcode

The intermediate result has these 8 columns. 6 columns from dbo.Customer and 2 columns from dbo.Zipinfo.

CustomerID	Name	Address	Zipcode	Gendercode	CustomertypeID	Zipcode	City
2	Irene Knudsen	Vestergade 13	8000	F	1	8000	Aarhus C
3	Claus Jensen	Torvet 13	6000	M	1	6000	Kolding
4	Per Larsen	Storegade 45	9000	M	1	9000	Aalborg
5	Hairdresser Tina	Lilletorv 17	5000	NULL	2	5000	Odense
6	Newsstand	Torvet 2	5000	NULL	2	5000	Odense
7	Jens Andersen	Havnegade 27	9000	NULL	1	9000	Aalborg
8	Ane Olsen	Vestergade 47	8000	F	1	8000	Aarhus C
9	Maren Kristensen	Strandvejen 111	8000	F	1	8000	Aarhus C

We can now join this intermidiate result table with the dbo.Customertype table because they both have the Customertype ID column and these columns can be used in the join condition. We add the third line as shown below. It is important to write the statement in a legible form - both to be understandable and to be easy to maintain.

```
SELECT     *
       FROM dbo.Customer  INNER JOIN dbo.Zipinfo         ON Customer.Zipcode = Zipinfo.Zipcode
                          INNER JOIN dbo.Customertype    ON Customer.CustomertypeID = Customertype.CustomertypeID;
```

CustomerID	Name	Address	Zipcode	Gendercode	CustomertypeID	Zipcode	City	Customer-typeID	Customer-typeTxt
2	Irene Knudsen	Vestergade 13	8000	F	1	8000	Aarhus C	1	Private
3	Claus Jensen	Torvet 13	6000	M	1	6000	Kolding	1	Private
4	Per Larsen	Storegade 45	9000	M	1	9000	Aalborg	1	Private
5	Hairdresser Tina	Lilletorv 17	5000	NULL	2	5000	Odense	2	Company
6	Newsstand	Torvet 2	5000	NULL	2	5000	Odense	2	Company
7	Jens Andersen	Havnegade 27	9000	NULL	1	9000	Aalborg	1	Private
8	Ane Olsen	Vestergade 47	8000	F	1	8000	Aarhus C	1	Private
9	Maren Kristensen	Strandvejen 111	8000	F	1	8000	Aarhus C	1	Private

We have all the data and can change * to the wanted columns. Again for readability we write the statement in the following way. Columns in the Projection is prefixed with the table name and with one column on each line.

```
SELECT     Customer.CustomerID,
           Customer.Name,
           Customer.Address,
           Customer.Zipcode,
           Zipinfo.City,
           Customertype.CustomertypeTxt
           FROM dbo.Customer  INNER JOIN dbo.Zipinfo         ON Customer.Zipcode = Zipinfo.Zipcode
                             INNER JOIN dbo.Customertype    ON Customer.CustomertypeID = Customertype.CustomertypeID;
```

The result is

CustomerID	Name	Address	Zipcode	City	CustomertypeTxt
2	Irene Knudsen	Vestergade 13	8000	Aarhus C	Private
3	Claus Jensen	Torvet 13	6000	Kolding	Private
4	Per Larsen	Storegade 45	9000	Aalborg	Private
5	Hairdresser Tina	Lilletorv 17	5000	Odense	Company
6	Newsstand	Torvet 2	5000	Odense	Company
7	Jens Andersen	Havnegade 27	9000	Aalborg	Private
8	Ane Olsen	Vestergade 47	8000	Aarhus C	Private
9	Maren Kristensen	Strandvejen 111	8000	Aarhus C	Private

In the above result we are 'missing' Customer with CustomerID = 1. Because the Customer's Zipcode is NULL there is no True match with any row in the table dbo.Zipinfo.

OUTER JOIN

We have three OUTER JOIN operations. These are LEFT, RIGHT and FULL JOIN. When we write the statement we can specify both LEFT JOIN and LEFT OUTER JOIN. It is just syntax. With and without OUTER specified, the same operation is performed. LEFT JOIN can only be a LEFT OUTER JOIN. By specifying OUTER we do not get a better understanding of the statement. I would never omit the word INNER from an INNER JOIN, even if the word JOIN alone is interpreted by the compiler as INNER JOIN. The question of JOIN type can be asked. It is about readability and maintainability.

In the sketch we use the operation LEFT JOIN and the join condition is an equi join. Therefore the operation is a LEFT EQUI JOIN.

With LEFT JOIN all rows from the left table are included in the result table even if there is no matching row from the right table.

The sketch above shows that all result rows from an INNER JOIN operation are part of the result table. These are the first four rows in the result table. When a row from the t1/LEFT table is compared to all the rows from t2, and all the comparisons evaluate to false, the t1 row is added to the result table with NULL for the t2 columns. In the example, this is the case for the t1 row, where f1 = 4.

For RIGHT JOIN we will use the same tables. We only show the result. The row with f3 = 13 is added to the result as a row without match with a t1 row. The columns f1 and f2 are NULL.

The first four rows in the sketch are the result of INNER JOIN. The fifth row is the result of the RIGHT join.

t1		t2		Result				Comment
f1	**f2**	**f3**	**f4**	**f1**	**f2**	**f3**	**f4**	SELECT * FROM t1 RIGHT JOIN t2 ON t1.f2 = t2.f4;
1	A	10	A	1	A	10	A	
2	A	11	B	2	A	10	A	
3	B	12	B	3	B	11	B	
4	F	13	C	3	B	12	B	
				NULL	NULL	13	C	

The next sketch is for FULL JOIN. In the sketch we start with the four rows that are the result from INNER JOIN. With FULL JOIN, both the rows from the left table t1 which have not been matched with a row from the right table, but also the rows from the right table t2 which have not been matched with a t1 row, are added to the result table. These are the result rows where f1 = 4 and f3 = 13 respectively.

t1		t2		Result				Comment
f1	**f2**	**f3**	**f4**	**f1**	**f2**	**f3**	**f4**	SELECT * FROM t1 FULL JOIN t2 ON t1.f2 = t2.f4;
1	A	10	A	1	A	10	A	
2	A	11	B	2	A	10	A	
3	B	12	B	3	B	11	B	
4	F	13	C	3	B	12	B	
				4	F	NULL	NULL	
				NULL	NULL	13	C	

Let's look at examples using the tables defined in the beginning of the chapter. When the INNER EQUI JOIN is performed we are missing CustermerID = 1. With the following query using the join operator LEFT JOIN all Customers are returned in the result.

```
SELECT      Customer.CustomerID,
            Customer.Name,
            Customer.Address,
            Customer.Zipcode,
            Zipinfo.City,
            Customer.Gendercode
            FROM dbo.Customer  LEFT JOIN dbo.Zipinfo          ON Customer.Zipcode = Zipinfo.Zipcode;
```

CustomerID	Name	Address	Zipcode	City	Gendercode
1	Peter Poulsen	NULL	NULL	NULL	NULL
2	Irene Knudsen	Vestergade 13	8000	Aarhus C	F
3	Claus Jensen	Torvet 13	6000	Kolding	M
4	Per Larsen	Storegade 45	9000	Aalborg	M
5	Hairdresser Tina	Lilletorv 17	5000	Odense	NULL
6	Newsstand	Torvet 2	5000	Odense	NULL
7	Jens Andersen	Havnegade 27	9000	Aalborg	NULL
8	Ane Olsen	Vestergade 47	8000	Aarhus C	F
9	Maren Kristensen	Strandvejen 111	8000	Aarhus C	F

From this result we can see that four of the nine Customers don't have a Gendercode. Maybe companies but in the example also persons, who are not telling the Gender. Again we use a LEFT JOIN for having translation of the Gendercode.

```
SELECT      Customer.CustomerID,
            Customer.Name,
            Customer.Address,
            Customer.Zipcode,
            Zipinfo.City,
            Customer.Gendercode,
            Gender.Gendertxt
            FROM dbo.Customer  LEFT JOIN dbo.Zipinfo          ON Customer.Zipcode = Zipinfo.Zipcode
                               LEFT JOIN dbo.Gender           ON Customer.Gendercode = Gender.Gendercode;
```

CustomerID	Name	Address	Zipcode	City	Gendercode	Gendertxt
1	Peter Poulsen	NULL	NULL	NULL	NULL	NULL
2	Irene Knudsen	Vestergade 13	8000	Aarhus C	F	Female
3	Claus Jensen	Torvet 13	6000	Kolding	M	Male
4	Per Larsen	Storegade 45	9000	Aalborg	M	Male
5	Hairdresser Tina	Lilletorv 17	5000	Odense	NULL	NULL
6	Newsstand	Torvet 2	5000	Odense	NULL	NULL
7	Jens Andersen	Havnegade 27	9000	Aalborg	NULL	NULL
8	Ane Olsen	Vestergade 47	8000	Aarhus C	F	Female
9	Maren Kristensen	Strandvejen 111	8000	Aarhus C	F	Female

Maybe together with the Customers we also want to see if there are Zipcode values where we don't have Customers - maybe there is a potential for sales.

With a FULL JOIN we can also get these Zipcode information included. It is important to include the Zipcode from dbo.Zipinfo and not from dbo.Customer. For both having CustomerID = 1 and the Zipcode 2000 and 4000 included we use a FULL JOIN.

```
SELECT    Customer.CustomerID,
          Customer.Name,
          Customer.Address,
          Zipinfo.Zipcode,
          Zipinfo.City,
          Customer.Gendercode
          FROM dbo.Customer  FULL JOIN dbo.Zipinfo        ON Customer.Zipcode = Zipinfo.Zipcode;
```

CustomerID	Name	Address	Zipcode	City	Gendercode
1	Peter Poulsen	NULL	NULL	NULL	NULL
2	Irene Knudsen	Vestergade 13	8000	Aarhus C	F
3	Claus Jensen	Torvet 13	6000	Kolding	M
4	Per Larsen	Storegade 45	9000	Aalborg	M
5	Hairdresser Tina	Lilletorv 17	5000	Odense	NULL
6	Newsstand	Torvet 2	5000	Odense	NULL
7	Jens Andersen	Havnegade 27	9000	Aalborg	NULL
8	Ane Olsen	Vestergade 47	8000	Aarhus C	F
9	Maren Kristensen	Strandvejen 111	8000	Aarhus C	F
NULL	NULL	NULL	2000	Frederiksberg	NULL
NULL	NULL	NULL	4000	Roskilde	NULL

We can mix the different join types as long as we remember that the precedence rules are from left to right. If we want to join all 4 tables, we need to know the following which is general knowledge of the system we are working with.

- only some of the Customers have a Zipcode.
- only some of the Customers have a Gendercode.
- all Customers have a Customertype value.

For the task we solve, we need to know if

- we want the not used Zipcodes.
- we want the not used Gender codes.
- we want the not used Customertype values.

```
SELECT    Customer.CustomerID,
          Customer.Name,
          Customer.Address,
          Zipinfo.Zipcode,
          Zipinfo.City,
          Gender.GenderTxt,
          Customertype.CustomertypeTxt
          FROM dbo.Customer  LEFT JOIN dbo.Zipinfo           ON Customer.Zipcode = Zipinfo.Zipcode
                             LEFT JOIN dbo.Gender            ON Customer.Gendercode = Gender.Gendercode
                             INNER JOIN dbo.Customertype     ON Customer.CustomertypeID = Customertype.CustomertypeID;
```

The result is

CustomerID	Name	Address	Zipcode	City	GenderTxt	CustomertypeTxt
1	Peter Poulsen	NULL	NULL	NULL	NULL	Private
2	Irene Knudsen	Vestergade 13	8000	Aarhus C	Female	Private
3	Claus Jensen	Torvet 13	6000	Kolding	Male	Private
4	Per Larsen	Storegade 45	9000	Aalborg	Male	Private
5	Hairdresser Tina	Lilletorv 17	5000	Odense	NULL	Company
6	Newsstand	Torvet 2	5000	Odense	NULL	Company
7	Jens Andersen	Havnegade 27	9000	Aalborg	NULL	Private
8	Ane Olsen	Vestergade 47	8000	Aarhus C	Female	Private
9	Maren Kristensen	Strandvejen 111	8000	Aarhus C	Female	Private

If we want all Zipcodes included in the result we can get a problem. We can try changing the first LEFT JOIN to FULL JOIN. This returns the same 9 rows in the result – not shown but look above. The conclusion could be that no Zipcodes exist without Customers. But we can see that no Customers is living in Zipcode 2000 or 4000.

```
SELECT      Customer.CustomerID,
            Customer.Name,
            Customer.Address,
            Zipinfo.Zipcode,
            Zipinfo.City,
            Gender.GenderTxt,
            Customertype.CustomertypeTxt
            FROM dbo.Customer FULL JOIN dbo.Zipinfo        ON Customer.Zipcode = Zipinfo.Zipcode
                              LEFT JOIN dbo.Gender         ON Customer.Gendercode = Gender.Gendercode
                              INNER JOIN dbo.Customertype  ON Customer.CustomertypeID = Customertype.CustomertypeID;
```

The problem is the rules of precedence. Because we join the dbo.Customer table with the dbo.Zipinfo table with the FULL JOIN operation, we end up with 11 rows. However, in this intermediate result, the CustomertypeID column is NULL for the rows with the missing Zipcodes. After joining this intermidiate result with the table dbo.CustomerType using an INNER JOIN the two rows with the missing Zipcodes is not included in the result.

If we use the following statement with * in the Projection, we can execute the first two lines by simply marking these lines, if the tool we are using allows this. It is possible in SSMS. We can also make the two last lines to comments. There are no columns in the Projection that prevent execution only a part of the statement, as no un-known columns are referenced. Therefore, * should be specified during development of the statement.

```
SELECT      *
            FROM dbo.Customer FULL JOIN dbo.Zipinfo        ON Customer.Zipcode = Zipinfo.Zipcode
                              LEFT JOIN dbo.Gender         ON Customer.Gendercode = Gender.Gendercode
                              INNER JOIN dbo.Customertype  ON Customer.CustomertypeID = Customertype.CustomertypeID;
```

In the result we have the two missing Zipcodes. But because the CustomertypeID is NULL for this rows the last join operation with an INNER JOIN excludes this rows from the result.

CustomerID	Name	Address	Zipcode	Gendercode	CustomertypeID	Zipcode	City
1	Peter Poulsen	NULL	NULL	NULL	1	NULL	NULL
...	...	...	...	...	...	...	...
9	Maren Kristensen	Strandvejen 111	8000	F	1	8000	Aarhus C
NULL	NULL	NULL	NULL	NULL	NULL	2000	Frederiksberg
NULL	NULL	NULL	NULL	NULL	NULL	4000	Roskilde

Knowing the precedence rules – from left to right – we can see that the last join operation must also be changed. With LEFT JOIN we keep all rows from the intermediate result.

```
SELECT      Customer.CustomerID,
            Customer.Name,
            Customer.Address,
            Zipinfo.Zipcode,
            Zipinfo.City,
            Gender.GenderTxt,
            Customertype.CustomertypeTxt
            FROM dbo.Customer FULL JOIN dbo.Zipinfo        ON Customer.Zipcode = Zipinfo.Zipcode
                              LEFT JOIN dbo.Gender         ON Customer.Gendercode = Gender.Gendercode
                              LEFT JOIN dbo.Customertype   ON Customer.CustomertypeID = Customertype.CustomertypeID;
```

CustomerID	Name	Address	Zipcode	City	GenderTxt	CustomertypeTxt
1	Peter Poulsen	NULL	NULL	NULL	NULL	Private
2	Irene Knudsen	Vestergade 13	8000	Aarhus C	Female	Private
3	Claus Jensen	Torvet 13	6000	Kolding	Male	Private
4	Per Larsen	Storegade 45	9000	Aalborg	Male	Private
5	Hairdresser Tina	Lilletorv 17	5000	Odense	NULL	Company
6	Newsstand	Torvet 2	5000	Odense	NULL	Company
7	Jens Andersen	Havnegade 27	9000	Aalborg	NULL	Private
8	Ane Olsen	Vestergade 47	8000	Aarhus C	Female	Private
9	Maren Kristensen	Strandvejen 111	8000	Aarhus C	Female	Private
NULL	NULL	NULL	2000	Frederiksberg	NULL	NULL
NULL	NULL	NULL	4000	Roskilde	NULL	NULL

Hopefully this shows that it's important to know the rules, but also to write the query in a way where the details can be easily evaluated during evaluation and corrected.

In the next example, we use BETWEEN in a Theta Join operation. We have a table with Persons whose ages are known. We want to group these Persons based on age. This could be groupings based on whether they are teen-agers, adults, retirees, etc. The wanted groupings are defined in the table dbo.AgeGroup. We have a column Age-GroupID but can of course add a column with a group name.

```
CREATE TABLE dbo.AgeGroup
(
        AgeGroupID      INT             NOT NULL
                        CONSTRAINT PK_AgeGroup
                        PRIMARY KEY,
        AgeFrom         SMALLINT        NOT NULL,
        AgeTo           SMALLINT        NOT NULL,

        CONSTRAINT CK_AgeGroup_AgeFrom_AgeTo
                CHECK (AgeFrom <= AgeTo)
);
```

```
CREATE TABLE dbo.Person
(
        PersonID        INT             NOT NULL
                        CONSTRAINT PK_Person PRIMARY KEY,
        Name            VARCHAR (20)    NOT NULL,
        Age             SMALLINT        NOT NULL
);
```

```
INSERT INTO dbo.AgeGroup (AgeGroupID, AgeFrom, AgeTo) VALUES
        (1, 0, 12),       (2, 13, 19),
        (3, 20, 68),      (4, 69, 90);
```

```
INSERT INTO dbo.Person (PersonID, Name, Age) VALUES
        (1,'Ida', 7),       (2, 'Tom', 12),      (3, 'Ane', 13),
        (10, 'Hans', 17),   (11, 'Mia', 19),
        (20, 'Karen', 34),  (21, 'Lars', 45),    (22, 'Jens', 55),
        (30, 'Maren', 77),  (31, 'Ruth', 82),    (32, 'Elvira', 99);
```

The join condition is a Theta Join because the person's age must be between the values in the AgeFrom and Age-To columns from the AgeGroup table. It is important to know that BETWEEN in SQL Server includes the FROM value and the TO value. BETWEEN is not seen in the execution plan because the compiler always change

        x BETWEEN 5 AND 10

to

        x >= 5 AND x <= 10

It is seen that CASE is used for this. But the solution with a table is more general. We can return more than one value and the information about the groups can maybe be changed by a user if we develop a dialog for this. If we use INNER JOIN and we have persons older than 90, these persons will be omitted from the result. Consider whether a LEFT JOIN should be used instead.

If we don't have a table, the following is a better solution than using CASE. In the following we use a row constructor and return two columns. CASE can only return one value.

```
SELECT  Person.PersonID,
        Person.Name,
        Person.Age,
        AgeGroup.AgeGroupID,
        AgeGroup.GroupTxt
        FROM dbo.Person LEFT JOIN (VALUES  (1, 0, 12, 'Child'),
                                           (2, 13, 19, 'Teens'),
                                           (3, 20, 68, 'Adult'),
                                           (4, 69, 90, 'Pensioner'))      AS AgeGroup (AgeGroupID, AgeFrom, AgeTo, GroupTxt)
        ON Person.Age BETWEEN AgeGroup.AgeFrom AND AgeGroup.AgeTo;
```

PersonID	Name	Age	AgeGroupID	GroupTxt
1	Ida	7	1	Child
2	Tom	12	1	Child
3	Ane	13	2	Teens
10	Hans	17	2	Teens
11	Mia	19	2	Teens
20	Karen	34	3	Adult
21	Lars	45	3	Adult
22	Jens	55	3	Adult
30	Maren	77	4	Pensioner
31	Ruth	82	4	Pensioner
32	Elvira	99	NULL	NULL

SELF JOIN

SELF JOIN is not a special Join type but one of the other types, but just where the two tables which are operand to the binary operation is the same table. We must still decide both Join Type and Join Condition. In the following, we have a table with both adults and children. The task is to list all Persons and for children, also the child's parents. We will use the same table three times.

Person AS PersonResult					Person AS PersonParent1					Person AS PersonParent2			
PersonID	Name	Parent1	Parent2		PersonID	Name	Parent1	Parent2		PersonID	Name	Parent1	Parent2
1	Ida	NULL	NULL		1	Ida	NULL	NULL		1	Ida	NULL	NULL
2	Tom	NULL	NULL		2	Tom	NULL	NULL		2	Tom	NULL	NULL
3	Ane	1	NULL		3	Ane	1	NULL		3	Ane	1	NULL
10	Hans	1	2		10	Hans	1	2		10	Hans	1	2
11	Mia	NULL	21		11	Mia	NULL	21		11	Mia	NULL	21
20	Karen	2	NULL		20	Karen	2	NULL		20	Karen	2	NULL
21	Lars	11	10		21	Lars	11	10		21	Lars	11	10
22	Jens	NULL	NULL		22	Jens	NULL	NULL		22	Jens	NULL	NULL

The following SELECT statement creates three logical copies of the same table. We don't care how it is implemented by the database system, only that we have three different references to the same table. So in our understanding and mindset we have three tables.

Since the same table is referenced multiple times, alias names should be used. I prefer that all versions of the table have an alias name that indicates the table's role in the statement. In the example, it is enough to use alias names for two of the tables. Do not use alias names like t1, t2, ... but use meaningful descriptive names. This increases understanding and maintainability.

The table from which all Persons are listed is giving the alias name PersonResult. If a row in this table has a value in the Parent1 column, we need to do a lookup in the PersonParent1 table. If the row has a value in the PersonParent2 column, we need to do a lookup in the PersonParent2 table. It is necessary to have two versions of these lookup tables as different values need to be looked up. Since both Parent1 and Parent2 columns can be NULL, the Join Type must be LEFT JOIN.

When PersonID = 10 is processed, a lookup of Parent1 = 1 must be made and also a lookup of Parent2 = 2. The tables and the SELECT statement is as following.

```
CREATE TABLE dbo.Person
(
        PersonID            INT                  NOT NULL
                            CONSTRAINT PK_Person PRIMARY KEY,
        Name                VARCHAR (20)         NOT NULL,
        Parent1             INT                  NULL
                            CONSTRAINT FK_Person_Parent1 FOREIGN KEY REFERENCES dbo.Person (PersonID),
        Parent2             INT                  NULL
                            CONSTRAINT FK_Person_Parent2 FOREIGN KEY REFERENCES dbo.Person (PersonID),
        CONSTRAINT CK_Person_Parent1_Parent2 CHECK (Parent1 <> Parent2)
);
```

```
GO
INSERT INTO dbo.Person (PersonID, Name, Parent1, Parent2) VALUES
        (1,'Ida', NULL, NULL),        (2, 'Tom', NULL, NULL),        (3, 'Ane', 1, NULL),
        (10, 'Hans', 1, 2),           (11, 'Mia', NULL, 21),          (20, 'Karen', 2, NULL),
        (21, 'Lars', 11, 10),         (22, 'Jens', NULL, NULL);
GO
SELECT    PersonResult.PersonID,
          PersonResult.Name,
          PersonParent1.Name        AS Parent1,
          PersonParent2.Name        AS Parent2
          FROM dbo.Person AS PersonResult  LEFT JOIN dbo.Person AS PersonParent1 ON PersonResult.Parent1 = PersonParent1.PersonID
                                           LEFT JOIN dbo.Person AS PersonParent2 ON PersonResult.Parent2 = PersonParent2.PersonID;
```

PersonID	Name	Parent1	Parent2
1	Ida	NULL	NULL
2	Tom	NULL	NULL
3	Ane	Ida	NULL
10	Hans	Ida	Tom
11	Mia	NULL	Lars
20	Karen	Tom	NULL
21	Lars	Mia	Hans
22	Jens	NULL	NULL

The conclusion is that a SELF JOIN is about having logical copies of the same table and then consider Join Type and Join Condition as we always do, when joining two different tables. In the above example we have three versions of the same table but just develop the statement as if we three tables.

CROSS JOIN

CROSS JOIN covers the mathematical concept Cartesian Product. The operation is binary and the result is all rows from one of the tables combined with all rows from the other table.

In the following example we use a table with Gender data and a table with AgeGroup information.

```
CREATE TABLE dbo.Gender
(
        Gendercode      CHAR (1)            NOT NULL
                        CONSTRAINT PK_Gender
                        PRIMARY KEY,
        GenderTxt       VARCHAR (20)       NOT NULL
);
```
```
CREATE TABLE dbo.AgeGroup
(
        AgeGroupID      INT        NOT NULL
                        CONSTRAINT PK_AgeGroup
                        PRIMARY KEY,
        AgeFrom         SMALLINT NOT NULL,
        AgeTo           SMALLINT NOT NULL,

        CONSTRAINT CK_AgeGroup_AgeFrom_AgeTo
                        CHECK (AgeFrom <= AgeTo)
);
```
```
INSERT INTO dbo.Gender (Gendercode, GenderTxt) VALUES
        ('F', 'Female'),    ('M', 'Male');
```
```
INSERT INTO dbo.AgeGroup (AgeGroupID, AgeFrom, AgeTo) VALUES
        (1, 0, 12),        (2, 13, 19),
        (3, 20, 68),       (4, 69, 90);
```

We want to create a report with all combinations of the values from the two tables. Because all combinations are not represented in the dbo.Person table used for the report, we must create a table with all these combinations.

```
SELECT    *
          FROM dbo.Gender CROSS JOIN dbo.AgeGroup;
```

Gendercode	GenderTxt	AgeGroupID	AgeFrom	AgeTo
F	Female	1	0	12
F	Female	2	13	19
F	Female	3	20	68
F	Female	4	69	90
M	Male	1	0	12
M	Male	2	13	19
M	Male	3	20	68
M	Male	4	69	90

It is important to note that this table implicitly has a Unique constraint on the combination of the columns Gendercode and AgeGroupID. These two columns are defined as PRIMARY KEY in each of the tables used as operands for the CROSS JOIN.

Later in the book, we show how we can use GROUP BY to count the number of rows for a group. Here we use the data created from such a statement. This table is Unique for the combination of the columns AgeGroupID and Gendercode. We name the table PersonAge.

AgeGroupID	Gendercode	Number
1	F	1
2	F	2
3	F	1
4	F	3
1	M	1
2	M	1
3	M	2

The table only contains seven rows. The combination of AgeGroup = 4 and Gendercode = 'M' is missing.

We use the table from the Cartesian Product and the dbo.PersonAge table to form the result. Because both tables have a composite Unique identifier, the Join Condition is an 'AND' combination of two expressions.

```
SELECT    Gender.GenderTxt,
          AgeGroup.AgeFrom,
          AgeGroup.AgeTo,
          PersonAge.Number
          FROM dbo.Gender    CROSS JOIN dbo.AgeGroup
                             LEFT JOIN dbo.PersonAge ON    AgeGroup.AgeGroupID = PersonAge.AgeGroupID    AND
                                                           Gender.Gendercode = PersonAge.Gendercode;
```

GenderTxt	AgeFrom	AgeTo	Number
Female	0	12	1
Female	13	19	2
Female	20	68	1
Female	69	90	3
Male	0	12	1
Male	13	19	1
Male	20	68	2
Male	69	90	NULL

From the result, we can see that we have no men in the age range from 69 to 90.

JOIN and Parentheses

In the following, we will look at how to develop a SELECT statement if we have many tables to use to solve the task. There are 9 tables, but only 3 objects/entities. When designing a database, we use normalization to minimize redundancy. We may choose to implement an object in multiple tables for performance or privilege reasons. All tables are in 4NF – Fourth Normal Form – so all tables are well-designed. All PRIMARY KEYS and FOREIGN KEYS are defined. In the sketches, only the necessary columns for each table are included. There is the following relationship between objects and tables.

Object/Entity	Tables
Customer	dbo.Region dbo.Zipinfo dbo.Customer
Product	dbo.Category dbo.SubCategory dbo.Product dbo.Employee
Order	dbo.OrderHeader dbo.OrderLine

In the following we are only looking at what we specify in FROM. We use parentheses for making it easier to choose the correct Join Type and easier to maintain and change the statement.

We look at the Customer object, which is implemented in three tables. These tables are defined as follows.

```
CREATE TABLE dbo.Region
(
        RegionID            SMALLINT            NOT NULL
                            CONSTRAINT PK_Region PRIMARY KEY,
        RegionName          VARCHAR (30)        NOT NULL
);

CREATE TABLE dbo.Zipinfo
(
        Zipcode             SMALLINT            NOT NULL
                            CONSTRAINT PK_Zipinfo PRIMARY KEY,
        City                VARCHAR (30)        NOT NULL,
        RegionID            SMALLINT            NOT NULL
                            CONSTRAINT FK_Zipinfo_Region FOREIGN KEY REFERENCES dbo.Region (RegionID)
);

CREATE TABLE dbo.Customer
(
        CustomerID          INT                 NOT NULL
                            CONSTRAINT PK_Customer PRIMARY KEY,
        Name                VARCHAR (30)        NOT NULL,
        Zipcode             SMALLINT            NULL
                            CONSTRAINT FK_Customer_Zipinfo FOREIGN KEY REFERENCES dbo.Zipinfo (Zipcode)
);
```

We can see that Customers do not always have a Zipcode, but that all Zipcodes point to a region.

If data about a Customer is to be included in a query, we must decide whether Zipinfo and Region data should be part of the result. We have the following alternatives.

	Comment	JOIN		
1	We can just use the dbo.Customer table	dbo.Customer		
2	If we want Zipinfo included we have two possibilities. Because Zipcode in Customer can be NULL we must use LEFT or RIGHT JOIN if all customers must be included. Both return the same result.	(dbo.Customer	LEFT JOIN dbo.Zipinfo ON Customer.Zipcode = Zipinfo.Zipcode)	
		(dbo.Zipinfo	RIGHT JOIN dbo.Customer ON Customer.Zipcode = Zipinfo.Zipcode)	
	If we only wants Customers having a Zipcode, INNER JOIN is used. The order of the tables does not matter.	(dbo.Customer	INNER JOIN dbo.Zipinfo ON Customer.Zipcode = Zipinfo.Zipcode)	
3	If we want data about the Region, we must also include Zipinfo. Both for the LEFT and the RIGHT JOIN from statement number 2 the join must be LEFT JOIN, because we have Customers without Zipcode. For INNER JOIN from statement number 2 we always have Zipinfo and then also a value for RegionID. Therefore INNER JOIN when joining with Region.	(dbo.Customer	LEFT JOIN dbo.Zipinfo ON Customer.Zipcode = Zipinfo.Zipcode LEFT JOIN dbo.Region ON Zipinfo.RegionID = Region.RegionID	
		(dbo.Customer	INNER JOIN dbo.Zipinfo ON Customer.Zipcode = Zipinfo.Zipcode INNER JOIN dbo.Region ON Zipinfo.RegionID = Region.RegionID)	

For Employee data we only have one table in this system – no problems.

The Product object/entity have up to four tables. These tables are defined as follows.

```
CREATE TABLE dbo.Category
(
        CategoryID          SMALLINT            NOT NULL
                            CONSTRAINT PK_Category PRIMARY KEY,
        CategoryName        VARCHAR (30)        NOT NULL
);
```

```
CREATE TABLE dbo.SubCategory
(
        SubCategoryID         SMALLINT            NOT NULL
                              CONSTRAINT PK_SubCategory PRIMARY KEY,
        SubCategoryName       VARCHAR (30)        NOT NULL,
        CategoryID            SMALLINT            NOT NULL
                              CONSTRAINT FK_SubCategory_Category FOREIGN KEY REFERENCES dbo.Category (CategoryID),
        ResponsEmp            INT                 NULL
                              CONSTRAINT FK_SubCategory_Emp FOREIGN KEY REFERENCES dbo.Employee (EmployeeID),
);

CREATE TABLE dbo.Product
(
        ProductID             INT                 NOT NULL
                              CONSTRAINT PK_Product PRIMARY KEY,
        ProductName           VARCHAR (30)        NOT NULL
                              CONSTRAINT UQ_Product_ProductName UNIQUE,
        UnitInStore           SMALLINT            NOT NULL DEFAULT (0)
                              CONSTRAINT CK_Product_AntalPaaLager CHECK (UnitInStore >= 0),
        SubCategoryID         SMALLINT            NOT NULL
                              CONSTRAINT FK_Product_Category FOREIGN KEY REFERENCES dbo.SubCategory (SubCategoryID),
);

CREATE TABLE dbo.Employee
(
        EmployeeID            INT                 NOT NULL
                              CONSTRAINT PK_Employee PRIMARY KEY,
        Name                  VARCHAR (30)        NOT NULL
);
```

As seen from the CREATE TABLE statements this tables gives less problems. All rows in Product reference a SubCategory row and all rows in the SubCategory table reference a Category row. The only problem is that if we want information about the Responsible Employee for a SubCategory, this information can be NULL.

	Comment	JOIN
1	We can use the Product table alone	dbo.Product
2	If we want information about the Product SubCategory we can use INNER JOIN as the column is defined with FOREIGN KEY and NOT NULL.	(dbo.Product INNER JOIN dbo.SubCategory ON Product.SubCategoryID = SubCategory.SubCategoryID)
3	If we want information about Category we must join Product – SubCategory – Category. Because the FOREIGN KEY columns are NOT NULL we can use INNER JOIN.	(dbo.Product INNER JOIN dbo.SubCategory ON Product.SubCategoryID = SubCategory.SubCategoryID INNER JOIN dbo.Category ON SubCategory.CategoryID = Category.CategoryID)
4	For statement number 3, we must join with LEFT JOIN if we also want data about the Responsible Employee. This also applies to statement number 2.	(dbo.Product INNER JOIN dbo.SubCategory ON Product.SubCategoryID = SubCategory.SubCategoryID INNER JOIN dbo.Category ON SubCategory.CategoryID = Category.CategoryID LEFT JOIN dbo.Employee ON SubCategory.ResponsEmp = Employee.EmployeeID)

The Order object/entity have two tables. These tables are defined as follows.

```
CREATE TABLE dbo.OrderHeader
(
        OrderID               INT                 NOT NULL
                              CONSTRAINT PK_OrderHeader PRIMARY KEY,
        CustomerID            INT                 NOT NULL
                              CONSTRAINT FK_OrderHeader_Customer FOREIGN KEY REFERENCES dbo.Customer (CustomerID)
);

CREATE TABLE dbo.OrderLine
(
        OrderID               INT                 NOT NULL
                              CONSTRAINT FK_OrderLine_OrderHeader FOREIGN KEY REFERENCES dbo.OrderHeader (OrderID),
        ProductID             INT                 NOT NULL
                              CONSTRAINT FK_OrderLine_Product FOREIGN KEY REFERENCES dbo.Product (ProductID),
```

```
        NumberOfUnits       SMALLINT         NOT NULL,

        CONSTRAINT PK_OrderLine PRIMARY KEY (OrderID, ProductID)
);
```

When we want the object/entity Order we do not have any problems because the FOREIGN KEY between the tables are NOT NULL and FOREIGN KEY defined.

When we develop a statement with some or all nine tables we can start with this sketch.

```
SELECT      *
        FROM      ( -- Customer -- )
                  JOIN
                  ( -- Order -- )
                  JOIN
                  ( -- Product -- )
```

We can then decide what Join Types should be used between these objects and at the same time figure out what the Join Condition should be. JOIN between OrderLine and Product will always be an INNER JOIN.

Only Customers that reference an Order. Only Order that reference a Customer	All Customers, including those without reference to an Order. All Orders including Orders without a reference to a Customer.	Only Customers, that reference an Order. All Orders including those without reference to a Customer.

`SELECT      *`
`    FROM    ( -- Customer -- )`
`    INNER JOIN`
`    ( -- Order -- )`
`    INNER JOIN`
`    ( -- Product -- )`
	`SELECT      *`
	`    FROM    ( -- Customer -- )`
	`    FULL JOIN`
	`    ( -- Order -- )`
	`    INNER JOIN`
	`    ( -- Product -- )`
		`SELECT      *`
		`    FROM    ( -- Customer -- )`
		`    RIGHT JOIN`
		`    ( -- Order -- )`
		`    INNER JOIN`
		`    ( -- Product -- )`

We can then use the outlines of the different object types and write these in the soft brackets. We most likely will not have these templates saved, but can build them according to the principles shown above. The interesting thing is that we only need to concentrate on the join type and conditions in one object/entity.

If we choose the following sketch

```
SELECT      *
        FROM      ( -- Customer -- )
                  INNER JOIN
                  ( -- Order -- )
                  INNER JOIN
                  ( -- Product -- )
```

we can 'translate' it to the following statement

```
SELECT      *
        FROM      (dbo.Customer      LEFT JOIN dbo.Zipinfo ON Customer.Zipcode = Zipinfo.Zipcode
                                     LEFT JOIN dbo.Region ON Zipinfo.RegionID = Region.RegionID)

                  INNER JOIN

                  (dbo.OrderHeader    INNER JOIN OrderLine ON OrderHeader.OrderID = OrderLine.OrderID)
                        ON Customer.CustomerID = OrderHeader.CustomerID

                  INNER JOIN

                  (dbo.Product        INNER JOIN dbo.SubCategory ON Product.SubCategoryID = SubCategory.SubCategoryID
                                      INNER JOIN dbo.Category ON SubCategory.CategoryID = Category.CategoryID)
                        ON OrderLine.ProductID = Product.ProductID;
```

or maybe to this one with fewer data. We do not include data from Zipinfo and Region when selecting Customer information. We exclude Category information about a Product.

```
SELECT   *
    FROM     dbo.Customer

             INNER JOIN

             (dbo.OrderHeader    INNER JOIN OrderLine ON OrderHeader.OrderID = OrderLine.OrderID)
                 ON Customer.CustomerID = OrderHeader.CustomerID

             INNER JOIN

             (dbo.Product        INNER JOIN dbo.SubCategory ON Product.SubCategoryID = SubCategory.SubCategoryID)
                 ON OrderLine.ProductID = Product.ProductID;
```

After developing the desired statement, we can replace * with the desired columns and optionally add how the data should be sorted. Of course, a WHERE clause can also be added.

If we want to change the last SELECT statement and add information about the Customer's City, it is a simple change. The consideration is about INNER or LEFT JOIN between dbo.Customer and dbo.Zipinfo, but not about joining with OrderHeader, Product, Category or …. This could easily be a problem if OUTER JOIN was used, but not in this statement as the precedence rules are controlled with parentheses for each object/entity. We just replace dbo.Customer with

```
SELECT   *
    FROM     (dbo.Customer      LEFT/INNER JOIN dbo.Zipinfo ON Customer.Zipcode = Zipinfo.Zipcode)
....
```

Note that there is no alias names specified for the result from the tables in the parentheses, so references in the Join Conditions and in the WHERE clause must be to the table and column names as they are defined in the database. Later we will look at Sub-Selects, where alias names are a requirement.

WHERE

In the WHERE clause it is possible to specify a condition that limits the number of rows in the result table. It is rare that all rows from a table have to be included in the result. It is important to keep in mind that a SELECT statement is a declarative statement where the conditions for the result are described and not a procedural statement where it is described step by step how the desired result is achieved. Therefore, it is important to know that selection conditions are specified under WHERE, and moving the condition to ON does not provide any performance improvements. The WHERE clause describes the selection conditions, and under ON, the join conditions are specified. A selection condition can be that only Customers from Zipcode = 5000 are included.

In the following we look at the WHERE clause. We use the following tables and data.

CREATE TABLE dbo.Zipinfo
(
   Zipcode   SMALLINT   NOT NULL
         CONSTRAINT PK_Zipinfo PRIMARY KEY,
   City   VARCHAR (20)   NOT NULL
);
	CREATE TABLE dbo.Gender
	(
	   Gendercode CHAR (1) NOT NULL
	         CONSTRAINT PK_Gender PRIMARY KEY,
	   GenderTxt VARCHAR (10) NOT NULL
	);

INSERT INTO dbo.Zipinfo (Zipcode, City) VALUES
   (2000, 'Frederiksberg'),   (4000, 'Roskilde'),
   (5000, 'Odense'),   (6000, 'Kolding'),
   (8000, 'Aarhus C'),   (9000, 'Aalborg');
	INSERT INTO dbo.Gender (Gendercode, GenderTxt) VALUES
	   ('F', 'Female'), ('M', 'Male');

CREATE TABLE dbo.Customer

(
   CustomerID   INT   NOT NULL
         CONSTRAINT PK_Customer PRIMARY KEY,
   Name   VARCHAR (35)   NOT NULL,
   Address   VARCHAR (35)   NULL,
   Zipcode   SMALLINT   NULL
         CONSTRAINT FK_Customer_Zipinfo FOREIGN KEY REFERENCES dbo.Zipinfo (Zipcode),
   Gendercode   CHAR (1)   NULL
         CONSTRAINT FK_Customer_Gender FOREIGN KEY REFERENCES dbo.Gender (Gendercode)
);

INSERT INTO dbo.Customer (CustomerID, Name, Address, Zipcode, Gendercode) VALUES
   (1, 'Peter Poulsen', NULL, NULL, NULL),   (2, 'Irene Knudsen', 'Vestergade 13', 8000, 'F'),
   (3, 'Claus Jensen', 'Torvet 13', 6000, 'M'),   (4, 'Per Larsen', 'Storegade 45', 9000, 'M'),
   (5, 'Hairdresser Tina', 'Lilletorv 17', 5000, NULL),   (6, 'Newsstand', 'Torvet 2', 5000, NULL),
   (7, 'Jens Andersen', 'Havnegade 27', 9000, NULL),   (8, 'Ane Olsen', 'Vestergade 47', 8000, 'F'),
   (9, 'Maren Kristensen', 'Strandvejen 111', 8000, 'F');

Simple Comparisons

We can specify simple comparisons between two expressions. The expression can be a constant, a column, or a calculation. The syntax is

expression { = | <> | > | >= | < | <= | != | !< | !> } expression

'!' means NOT but is rarely used. Instead of != use <> and instead of !< use >=. It is mostly used by developers who have learned other programming languages where it is used.

Zipcode = 2000	Firstname = 'Ole'	CreateDate > DATEADD (DAY, -7, SYSDATETIME ())
Zipcode > 5000	Gender = 'M'	Zipcode / 1000 <> 3
LEFT (Firstname, 1) = 'K'	1 = 1	LEFT (Firstname, 1) = LEFT (Lastname, 1)

The following two expressions are exactly the same expressions, both the calculations and the comparisons. But try to write the expression in the most reader-friendly way. Some expressions can be read without stopping in the middle of a statement and starting over. This often provides the best understanding. For me, the first one is the most readable.

WHERE Amount * TaxPct / 100 > 1000	WHERE 1000 < Amount * TaxPct / 100

When comparing two values be sure that the data types of the two values are equal.

When calculating with integer values, for example when calculating 25% tax, it is important how the expression is written. The intermediate result from the calculation is also an integer data type, therefore decimal values are truncated. Rounding up or down is not done automatically. We are looking at an amount of 27, the value in the column IntValue.

27 divided by 100 is 0.27 but truncated to 0. 0 multiplied with 25 is 0. If we look at the other way of writing the formula we first multiply 25 with 27 giving 675. When we divide by 100 the result is 6.75 but truncated to 6.

IntValue / 100 * 25 = 0	IntValue * 25 / 100 = 6

We change the formulas to the following where 100 is changed to 100.0. This constant have the data type DECIMAL because of the decimal point. We now have both integer and decimal data types in the calculation. The result data type is the decimal data type and then the same result from both calculation.

IntValue / 100.0 * 25 = 6.75	IntValue * 25 / 100.0 = 6.75

Instead of using 100.0, we could use the CAST function. The function CAST converts from one data type to another data type. But this can still cause problems.

IntValue / 100 * CAST (25 AS DECIMAL (9,2)) = 0

will still give the result 0. First, IntValue is divided by 100. Both values have the data type integer, so the result also has the data type integer. Only when this 0 which is an integer is multiplied by the decimal data type 25.0 - CAST (25 AS DECIMAL (9,2)) - does the result become a decimal number. But that is too late. Convert the first or second value in the expression. SQL Server evaluates and executes an expression from left to right if there is equal precedence.

If the data type of the DecValue column is DECIMAL (9,2), the results for the two calculation methods are the same because the first calculation in the expression is with decimal data types. Therefore, all intermediate results have the DECIMAL data type. However, the result is different than for the INTEGER data type. Therefore, it can be a problem to compare values where the data types used in the calculation are different.

DecValue / 100 * 27 = 6.750000	DecValue * 27 / 100 = 6.750000

BETWEEN Value AND Value

With BETWEEN it is evaluated whether a column, expression, or constant is greater than or equal to value1 and less than or equal to value2. This means that the value is in a range.

- Column   BETWEEN value1 AND value2
- Expression   BETWEEN value1 AND value2
- Constant   BETWEEN value1 AND value2

Value1 and Value2 can be an expression or even a Sub-Select as described later in the book.

To compare, the data type of the column, expression, constant, value1, and value2 must be one of the Scalar data types. The rules for the scalar data types are that there is a limited number of allowed values, and that these values are ordered/comparable. Scalar data types are all of the integer data types, the decimal data type, the various string types, and the date and time data types.

BETWEEN are not known after compiling of the statement. We cannot find BETWEEN in the execution plan

Zipcode BETWEEN 6000 AND 8000

is changed when compiled to

```
Zipcode >= 6000 AND Zipcode <= 8000
```

This shows that the smallest value according to the Scalar data type should be Value1 and the same or a greater value should be Value2. It also shows that the specified values are included in the range. If the greatest value is specified first the condition is a nonsense expression but still evaluated.

The Non-Scalar data types are XML or the geography data type, which contains latitude and longitude. It is not relevant to compare longitude/latitude for Copenhagen and Paris. Which one has the greatest value?

If we are comparing date/datetime values, we should use the date format 'yyyy-mm-dd' for the day. If we are using the format 'mm-dd-yyyy', it can be mixed with 'dd-mm-yyyy' if we are using the value '2024-08-01'. We can also use one of the date functions as in the following.

```
SELECT    Date
          FROM dbo.t
          WHERE Date BETWEEN DATEADD (DAY, -14, SYSDATETIME ())  AND  SYSDATETIME ();
```

NOT BETWEEN specifies that the valid values must be outside the range to be true. NOT can be specified in two ways, as shown below. Use the first to have a readable statement.

```
SELECT    *
          FROM dbo.Zipinfo
          WHERE Zipcode NOT BETWEEN 6000 AND 8000;

SELECT    *
          FROM dbo. Zipinfo
          WHERE NOT Zipcode BETWEEN 6000 AND 8000;
```

Both will be changed to

```
Zipcode < 6000 AND Zipcode > 8000
```

Even the following condition

```
NOT Zipcode NOT BETWEEN 6000 AND 8000;
```

is changed to the following when compiled. This shows that trying all possible tricks doesn't help. A lot gets changed when the statement is compiled.

```
Zipcode BETWEEN 6000 AND 8000;
```

and then to

```
Zipcode >= 6000 AND Zipcode <= 8000
```

The following condition is ignored – but allowed – because it is a nonsense expression.

```
SELECT    *
          FROM dbo. Zipinfo
          WHERE 7000 BETWEEN 6000 AND 8000;
```

For the following statement the condition is ignored because it is a nonsense expression which always evaluate to false. No data is selected.

```
SELECT    *
          FROM dbo.Person
          WHERE Zipcode BETWEEN 8000 AND 6000;
```

IN (Value1, Value2, Value3)

IN evaluates whether a column, expression, or constant is equal to one of the listed values in the comma separated list of values. IN is an =/equi evaluation against alternative values.

- Column   IN (Value1, Value2, ...)
- Expression   IN (Value1, Value2, ...)
- Constant   IN (Value1, Value2, ...)

The compiler also modifies an expression with IN. The values are sorted and duplicates are removed.

```
SELECT    *
          FROM dbo.Zipinfo
          WHERE Zipcode IN (6000, 8000, 2000);
```

After compilation, the expression is changed to the following. IN is not shown in the execution plan because IN is changed to OR. The values are ordered

```
Zipcode = 2000 OR Zipcode = 6000 OR Zipcode = 8000
```

Some programming languages recommend that in expressions with OR, the value with the most hits is specified first. This is not true for SQL Server, as the values are sorted by their scalar sort order. The same applies if the statement uses the OR construct instead of IN. The values are still sorted and result in a condition as above.

```
SELECT    *
          FROM dbo.Zipinfo
          WHERE    Zipcode = 8000    OR
                   Zipcode = 2000    OR
                   Zipcode = 6000;
```

With the following statement, we have the same condition as above after compilation - values are ordered and duplicates removed.

```
SELECT    *
          FROM dbo.Zipinfo
          WHERE Zipcode IN (6000, 8000, 2000, 8000, 2000, 8000, 2000, 8000, 2000, 8000, 2000, 8000, 2000);
```

The following combination of OR and =/equal are reduced to evaluate for 1000, 2000, 3000, 4000, 6000, 8000 and 9000. Again an example that shows that it is not possible to cheat the compiler.

```
SELECT    *
          FROM dbo.Zipinfo
          WHERE    Zipcode = 8000    OR
                   Zipcode = 2000    OR
                   Zipcode = 9000    OR
                   Zipcode IN (2000, 4000, 6000, 3000, 1000);
```

If we insert NULL into the value list, NULL is ignored. Not because NULL is not a value, but because the transformation is only to

```
Column = Value
```

When working with NULL in a column, this condition is false and should instead be

```
Column IS NULL
```

Microsoft has chosen not to 'help', so the following construction should be used instead.

```
Column IN (Value1, Value2, Value3) OR Column IS NULL
```

The condition is transformed to

```
Column IS NULL OR Column = Value1 OR Column = Value2 OR Column = Value3
```

If the referenced column is defined with NOT NULL, the expression "Column IS NULL" is ignored. It is the first evaluation and will be expensive because it will always evaluate to false - it will just be a waste of time.

NOT IN indicates that it must not be one of the listed values for the condition to be true. As with BETWEEN we can use the following two ways of including NOT in the expression.

SELECT   *
     FROM dbo.Zipinfo
     WHERE Zipcode NOT IN (6000, 8000, 2000);
	SELECT *
	     FROM dbo.Zipinfo
	     WHERE NOT Zipcode IN (6000, 8000, 2000);

Both conditions will be transformed to

Zipcode <> 2000 AND Zipcode <> 6000 AND Zipcode <> 8000

LIKE

LIKE compares a column or expression to a pattern that includes wildcards. If no wildcards are included in the pattern, the =/equal operator should be used instead of.

- Column   LIKE pattern
- Expression   LIKE pattern

With the LIKE operator, the column or expression must be one of the string data types.

The valid wildcards in the pattern are

%	with %/percent there can be 0 or any number of characters at this position.
_ (underscore)	with _/underscore there must be exact one character at the position.
[bdfg]	with characters in square brackets, any single character at the position must be within the specified set of characters. If a set is specified the characters are listed without comma or space between and in any order.
[b-g]	if '-' is specified, it means that a range of values is allowed. With a range, the lowest value must be first in the sort order.
[^]	with specification of ^ as the first character in a set or range, the character must not be among the specified characters in the range or set.

Range and set can be combined in the same specification.

If we want to evaluate if the value in a string column is 8 digits, we can use LIKE. In Denmark all telephone numbers are 8 digits. The number '12345678' is valid but '12 34 56 78' is wrong. We always use 8 digits.

    TelephoneNumber LIKE '[0-9][0-9][0-9][0-9][0-9][0-9][0-9][0-9]'

We are sure that there are 8 digits and all in the value range from 0 to 9.

The two Firstname values Peter and Peder are very similar as Carl/Karl and Carsten/Karsten. If we need to find a person with one of these names we can use the following LIKE expression. In the example we do not know the Lastname so % is specified.

    WHERE Name LIKE 'Pe[dt]er%'

In the third position we can have the letter "d" or "t". With % last we can have any Lastname, even no Lastname. As for BETWEEN and IN we can combine LIKE with NOT.

It is important to focus on the fact that these are alternative values at one position. We cannot use this for searching if it is Christina/Kristina, where it is Ch contra K.

IS NULL

If a Column or Expression is NULL, the condition must be specified as 'IS NULL' and not as '= NULL'. Column = NULL is always false.

If we want to select all Customers with an unknown address we can use the following statement. Both the column Street and the column Zipcode is evaluated. A Street without a Zipcode or a Zipcode without a Street is not useful. Both columns must be defined allowing NULL.

```
SELECT      *
        FROM dbo.Customer
        WHERE    Street      IS NULL    OR
                 Zipcode     IS NULL;
```

As for BETWEEN, IN and LIKE we can combine IS NULL with NOT as

```
        Column IS NOT NULL
```

Sometimes an empty string is used instead of NULL. So even the column accepts NULL an empty string is inserted. We can then use the Function NULLIF in the expression.

```
        NULLIF (Column, '') IS NULL
```

AND, OR and Parenthesis

Logical expressions can be combined with AND/OR, to form a new Logical expression. With parentheses we can change the precedence rules. but also use it for simply make an expression more understandable. This is especially interesting if we use both AND and OR.

With AND, both logical expressions must be true for the entire expression to be true. With expressions combined with OR, one or both of the logical expressions must be true for the entire expression to be true. The precedence rules for AND and OR are that AND is the strongest, i.e. it is executed first.

Above we saw that BETWEEN was converted to two expressions combined with AND. For IN, the compiler change each value in the value list to an expression and combined these with OR.

When we join two tables we can have join columns that must contain NULL. In the following we have a table with Customers and a table with the CustomerType. Maybe the CustomerType is Unknown and we do not want to insert an 'U'/Unknown or another value but use NULL. In dbo.CustomerType table the column CustomerTypeID is not defined as PRIMARY KEY but as UNIQUE. The UNIQUE constraint allows one row with NULL in the column.

```
CREATE TABLE dbo.CustomerType
(
        CustomerTypeID      CHAR (1)            NULL
                            CONSTRAINT UQ_CustomerType_CustomerType UNIQUE,
        CustomerTypeName VARCHAR (10)       NOT NULL
);

CREATE TABLE dbo.Customer
(
        CustomerID          INT                NOT NULL
                            CONSTRAINT PK_Customer PRIMARY KEY,
        Name                VARCHAR (30)       NOT NULL,
        CustomerTypeID      CHAR (1)           NULL
                            CONSTRAINT FK_Customer_CustomerType FOREIGN KEY REFERENCES dbo.CustomerType (CustomerTypeID)
);
```

We insert four CustomerTypes and four Customers.

```
INSERT INTO dbo.CustomerType (CustomerTypeID, CustomerTypeName) VALUES
          (NULL, 'Unknown'),   ('C', 'Company'),      ('F', 'Female'),        ('M', 'Male');

INSERT INTO dbo.Customer (CustomerID, Name, CustomerTypeID) VALUES
          (1, 'Company1', 'C'),   (2, 'Jensen', NULL),   (3, 'Ida Olsen', 'F'),   (4, 'Hans Andersen', 'M');
```

The task is to list all Customers. The following Join Condition is not correct because NULL = NULL is false. It is not syntactic correct to specify t1.Column1 IS t2.Column2.

```
SELECT      *
          FROM dbo.Customer INNER JOIN dbo.CustomerType
                  ON Customer.CustomerTypeID = CustomerType.CustomerTypeID;
```

CustomerID	Name	CustomerTypeID	CustomerTypeID	CustomerTypeName
1	Company1	C	C	Company
3	Ida Olsen	F	F	Female
4	Hans Andersen	M	M	Male

The join condition for the INNER JOIN is as follows. We compare values with the expression

Customer.CustomerTypeID = CustomerType.CustomerTypeID

and match NULL with NULL in the join condition with the expression

(Customer.CustomerTypeID IS NULL   AND   CustomerType.CustomerTypeID IS NULL)

Because we use both OR and AND we also use parenthesis. The parenthesis is not necessary because AND is stronger than OR, but used for readability.

```
SELECT      *
          FROM dbo.Customer INNER JOIN dbo.CustomerType
                  ON        Customer.CustomerTypeID = CustomerType.CustomerTypeID              OR
                        (Customer.CustomerTypeID IS NULL  AND  CustomerType.CustomerTypeID IS NULL);
```

CustomerID	Name	CustomerTypeID	CustomerTypeID	CustomerTypeName
1	Company1	C	C	Company
2	Jensen	NULL	NULL	Unknown
3	Ida Olsen	F	F	Female
4	Hans Andersen	M	M	Male

The following statement shows one way to solve the problem. If the column is NULL, we change NULL to the value '!' in both tables while performing the join operation. This way we get a translation of CustomerTypeID NULL to the text 'Unknown'. Make sure that the replacement value is a value that will never be used as a legal value in the future. In the example, '!' is used.

```
SELECT      *
          FROM dbo.Customer INNER JOIN dbo.CustomerType
                  ON COALESCE (Customer.CustomerTypeID, '!') = COALESCE (CustomerType.CustomerTypeID, '!');
```

Starting with SQL Server version 2022, we have a new option called the 'IS NOT DISTINCT FROM' operator. Using this, NULL = NULL evaluates to true. It will not be discussed further in this book.

```
SELECT      *
          FROM dbo.Customer INNER JOIN dbo.CustomerType
                  ON Customer.CustomerTypeID IS NOT DISTINCT FROM CustomerType.CustomerTypeID;
```

Both the use of COALESCE and 'IS NOT DISTINCT FROM' give the correct result for the task where all Customers are included in the result and NULL in CustomerTypeID is translated correctly to 'Unknown'.

Both the use of COALESCE and 'IS NOT DISTINCT FROM' give the correct result. CustomerTypeID is translated correct. It is important that the value is selected from a table and not translated using a CASE statement or is a constant in one of the functions ISNULL or COALESCE. By retrieving the value from a table, the language can be changed or we can choose to translate to 'n/a' instead of 'Unknown'.

GROUP BY

If we want to count the number of employees or count the number of customers in each zip code, we can use GROUP BY. With GROUP BY, we reduce the number of result rows by grouping all rows with the same value into one row in the result. There must be one or more columns in the table that have the same value for multiple rows. The result table will have fewer rows than the input table. It is allowed/possible for the entire table to be one group, resulting in one row in the result table.

Grouping on a PRIAMRY KEY or UNIQUE column is not relevant and will be ignored by SQL Server. No error will be returned, but there will be the same number of rows in the result table as in the table the data is read from.

In addition to the column(s) being grouped on, one or more aggregation functions can be included in the result. The most commonly used is

COUNT (*)	Returns the number of rows in the group.
COUNT (DISTINCT Expressions)	If the Expression is a column we count the number of different values in the column.
COUNT (Expression)	Returns the number of rows in a group where Expression is not NULL. Expressions can be of any data type.
SUM (Expression)	Returns the sum of the values in the Expression of the group. Expressions must be a numeric data type.
AVG (Expression)	Returns the average of the values in the Expression of the group. Expressions must be a numeric data type.
MIN (Expression)	Returns the smallest of the values in the Expression of the group. Expressions must be a scalar data type.
MAX (Expression)	Returns the largest value in the Expression of the group. Expressions must be a scalar data type.

It is not giving a better performance by specifying COUNT (1) or COUNT (PRIMARY KEY) than specifying COUNT (*). In SQL Server all three construction will result in the same execution plan. We will take a look at the aggregation function COUNT and use the following dbo.Person table.

```
CREATE TABLE dbo.Person
(
        ID              INT                 NOT NULL,
        Name            VARCHAR (30)        NOT NULL,
        Address         VARCHAR (30)        NULL,
        Zipcode         SMALLINT            NULL
);
```

ID	Name	Address	Zipcode
1	Ole	Nygade 4	2000
2	Fie	Torvet 11	4000
3	Per	Strandvejen 3	5000
4	Bo	Borgergade 44	2000
5	Hanne	NULL	NULL
6	Bo	Nygade 22	2000
7	Fie	Torvet 11	4000
8	Erik	NULL	NULL
9	Fie	Overgaden 11	4000

```
SELECT    COUNT (*)                   AS NumberOfPersons,
          COUNT (Zipcode)             AS NumberOfZipcodeValues,
          COUNT (DISTINCT Zipcode)    AS NumberOfDiffZipcode
          FROM dbo.Person;
```

We do not specify GROUP BY, and the table is therefore one group. We only have columns in the result that are the result of an aggregation function. The statement will return 9 from COUNT (*) because we have 9 rows in the table. COUNT (Zipcode) returns 7 because two of the rows has NULL in the Zipcode column or, in another way, there are 7 rows that have a value. The last COUNT (DISTINCT Zipcode) returns 3 because we have 3 different values in the column. NULL is not a value. I never use the expression a NULL-value.

NumberOfPersons	NumberOfZipcodeValues	NumberOfDiffZipcode
9	7	3

We can GROUP BY the column Zipcode. This is relevant because the column only have 3 values and NULL in a table with 9 rows.

```
SELECT    Zipcode,
          COUNT (*)           AS Number
          FROM dbo.Person
          GROUP BY Zipcode;
```

Zipcode	Number
NULL	2
2000	3
4000	3
5000	1

This shows that we in the result has 3 rows with the different values in the column and one row with NULL. All rows in the table are counted. The following statement will return an error when compiled and never be executed.

```
SELECT    Zipcode,
          Name,
          COUNT (*) AS Number
          FROM dbo.Person
          GROUP BY Zipcode;
```

Msg 8120, Level 16, State 1, Line 41
Column 'dbo.Person.Name' is invalid in the select list because it is not contained in either an aggregate function or the GROUP BY clause.

It is logical why the Name column cannot be a column in the Projection. For each Zipcode value we can have multiple Name values. For Zipcode = 2000 we have the Name values Ole and Bo. Which should be shown in the result? We need to be precise because SQL Server will not choose. The following statement is correct because it is unambiguous which name value should be displayed. MAX of the values Ole and Bo is Ole.

```
SELECT    Zipcode,
          MAX (Name)          AS Name,
          COUNT (*)           AS Number
          FROM dbo.Person
          GROUP BY Zipcode;
```

Zipcode	Name	Number
...	...	...
2000	Ole	3
...	...	...

Note that there are not 3 people named Ole in Zipcode 2000, but 3 people in Zipcode 2000. We do not know the names, only that the largest in alphabetical order is Ole. Be careful not to create a result that can be misunderstood.

We can GROUP BY on more than one column. In the following, the GROUP BY columns are Zipcode and Name. The result shows that there are two persons in Zipcode = 2000 named Bo and in Zipcode = 4000 all are named Fie. The result is not ordered. If we want the result sorted in a specific way, we need to add ORDER BY to the statement. The result is very similar to the result above, but gives completely different information.

```
SELECT    Zipcode,
          Name,
          COUNT (*) AS Number
          FROM dbo.Person
          GROUP BY Zipcode, Name;
```

Zipcode	Name	Number
2000	Bo	2
NULL	Erik	1
4000	Fie	3
NULL	Hanne	1
2000	Ole	1
5000	Per	1

The next example focuses on the aggregation functions SUM, AVG, MIN, and MAX. We will use the following table. The table can be the result of aggregating data from tables such as dbo.OrderHeader and dbo.OrderLine. Later, we look at views and CTEs that can be used for a task like this. The definition of the dbo.CustomerSale is

```
CREATE TABLE dbo.CustomerSale
(
        ID                  INT       NOT NULL       IDENTITY
                                      CONSTRAINT PK_CustomerSale PRIMARY KEY,
        CustomerID          INT       NOT NULL,
        OrderID             INT       NOT NULL,
        OrderDate           DATE      NOT NULL,
        Amount              INT       NOT NULL,
        Discount            INT       NULL

        CONSTRAINT UQ_CustomerSale UNIQUE (CustomerID, OrderID)
);
```

ID	CustomerID	OrderID	OrderDate	Amount	Discount
1	1	234	2024-04-09	4900	400
2	1	811	2024-05-10	500	NULL
3	1	934	2024-06-03	650	NULL
4	1	1021	2024-07-18	350	NULL
5	1	1233	2024-10-28	1700	200
6	3	111	2024-05-11	300	30
7	3	674	2024-08-16	950	90
8	3	812	2024-10-21	750	60
9	8	48	2023-11-26	700	45
10	8	122	2024-08-31	150	NULL
11	8	588	2024-09-20	250	25
12	8	608	2024-11-23	100	5
13	9	47	2024-04-05	2	NULL
14	9	56	2024-04-08	1	NULL

In the first statement, we look at each Customer individually. We want to summarize the amount for each year for each Customer. For the Year column, we use the YEAR function on the OrderDate column.

CustomerID	Year	Total
1	2024	8100
3	2024	2000
8	2023	700
8	2024	500
9	2024	3

```
SELECT    CustomerID,
          YEAR (OrderDate)              AS Year,
          SUM (Amount)                  AS Total
          FROM dbo.CustomerSale
          GROUP BY CustomerID, YEAR (OrderDate)
          ORDER BY CustomerID, Year;
```

We can see from the statement that the alias name Year for the calculated column in the Projection/select list is used in ORDER BY but not in GROUP BY. It is a rule in SQL Server and a choice from Microsoft that the alias name only can be used in ORDER BY and not in GROUP BY.

Next, we look at the aggregation function AVG. We will calculate the average in different ways. It is important to focus on the data types. Both the Amount column and the Discount column are integers. With this data type, the result value is also an integer. To see what the result value would be if the data types were DECIMAL instead of integer, we convert the value in the columns to DECIMAL (9, 2) using the CAST function.

```
SELECT    CustomerID,
          AVG (Amount)                                        AS Col1,
          SUM (CAST (Amount AS DECIMAL (9, 2))) / COUNT (*)   AS Col2,
          AVG (Discount)                                      AS Col3,
          SUM (Discount) / COUNT (Discount)                   AS Col4,
          SUM (Discount) / COUNT (*)                          AS Col5,
          SUM (CAST (Discount AS DECIMAL (9, 2))) / COUNT (*) AS Col6
          FROM dbo.CustomerSale
          GROUP BY CustomerID;
```

We can see that there is a difference between the result value in Col1 and Col2 for CustomerID = 9. The two integer values using when calculating the average are the values 1 and 2. The average is 1.5, but because the Amount column used in Col1 has the data type integer, the result is 1. For Col2, the result has 6 decimal places, but can be converted to only 2 decimal places with CAST. The most important thing is that the result is 1.5. Depending on the data and the task, we need to decide whether to convert integers.

CustomerID	Col1	Col2	Col3	Col4	Col5	Col6
1	1620	1620.000000	300	300	120	120.000000
3	666	666.666666	60	60	60	60.000000
8	300	300.000000	25	25	18	18.750000
9	1	1.500000	NULL	NULL	NULL	NULL

If we look at Col3, Col4 and Col5 for CustomerID = 8 we have different result values. We use the Discount column. Three rows have a value – 5, 25 and 45 – and one row is NULL. For Col3 the rule for the function is used. The 3 values are summed, giving 75, and because we have three values, the result is 75 / 3 = 25.

For Col4, we use the SUM aggregation function, which returns 75. By using the COUNT function with a column, only the columns values are counted, not rows with NULL. This is the same as using the AVG function, and returns 25. For Col5, the sum is still 75, but we count rows with COUNT (*). The result is 75 / 4 = 18.75, but because the data type is an integer, the result is 18.

We can use MAX and MIN for returning the biggest Amount and the smallest Amount. If Amount is the value after subtraction of Discount we can find MAX and MIN before Discount is subtracted. Because Discount can be NULL and adding NULL to a value gives NULL, we must use the COALESCE function for changing NULL to 0. This shows that we can specify an expression as parameter to the aggregation functions.

```
SELECT    CustomerID,
          MAX (Amount + COALESCE (Discount, 0))    AS MaxAmount,
          MIN (Amount + COALESCE (Discount, 0))    AS MinAmount
          FROM dbo.CustomerSale
          GROUP BY CustomerID;
```

CustomerID	MaxAmount	MinAmount
1	5300	350
3	1040	330
8	745	105
9	2	1

It also shows that by using NULL instead of 0, we can decide for this task whether we want the average of the Orders where a Discount has been given or we want an average calculated over all Orders. For Avg1 and Avg2 it is the average for Orders with an Discount value. For Avg3 and Avg4 it is in relation to all Orders. Using the function COALESCE for Avg3 all rows have a value since NULL is changed to 0.

```
SELECT    AVG (Discount)                          AS Avg1,
          SUM (Discount) / COUNT (Discount)       AS Avg2,
          AVG (COALESCE (Discount, 0))            AS Avg3,
          SUM (Discount) / COUNT (*)              AS Avg4
          FROM dbo.CustomerSale;
```

Avg1	Avg2	Avg3	Avg4
106	106	61	61

If we ORDER BY a column allowing NULL, NULL will come first, but MIN (Col) returns the first value and NULL is not a value. Therefore the following statement returns 5.

```
SELECT    MIN (Discount)
          FROM dbo.CustomerSale;
```

HAVING

HAVING allows for adding rules to the intermediate result created based on GROUP BY. Maybe we want to look at data from Zipcodes where we have more than 100 customers. Maybe we want to look at data about families with more than 10 children. HAVING can only be used in a statement with GROUP BY.

We must distinguish between conditions under WHERE and conditions under HAVING. We must remember that the statement is a declarative statement, where everything described in the statement is analysed before the execution plan is generated. The compiler will generate exactly the same execution plan for Statement 1 and 2 below. Logically, Statement 2 is an incorrect statement but syntactically correct.

All the conditions related to and limiting the rows to be included in the grouping operation should be specified in the WHERE clause, for example Zipcode BETWEEN 6000 AND 9000. With HAVING we specify conditions on the intermediate result after grouping of the rows selected after filtering by the condition in the WHERE clause. In HAVING, an aggregate value should be referenced in the condition, as this can only be done after the grouping and calculation of an aggregate value. In the statement below, it is COUNT (*) > 1000.

The third statement gives a compilation error because a condition with a reference to an aggregate function is syntactically only allowed in HAVING and not in the WHERE clause.

```
-- 1      the correct version
SELECT   Zipcode,
         COUNT (*)            AS Number
         FROM dbo.Person
         WHERE Zipcode BETWEEN 6000 AND 9000
         GROUP BY Zipcode
         HAVING COUNT (*) > 1000;
-- 2      works, but not logical correct
SELECT   Zipcode,
         COUNT (*)            AS Number
         FROM dbo.Person
         GROUP BY Zipcode
         HAVING   COUNT (*) > 1000           AND
                  Zipcode BETWEEN 6000 AND 9000;
-- 3      syntax error
SELECT   Zipcode,
         COUNT (*)            AS Number
         FROM dbo.Person
         WHERE   COUNT (*) > 1000            AND
                 Zipcode BETWEEN 6000 AND 9000
         GROUP BY Zipcode;
```

The following sketch shows what the different clauses in the statement mean for the intermediate and final result.

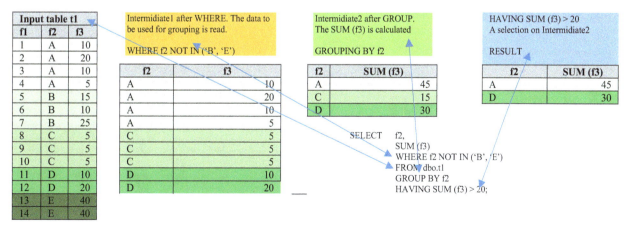

Statement 3 gives the following compilation error.

From the sketch we can see that the filter expression in WHERE is used before grouping/GROUP BY. When the rows are read from the table, an index may be used to filter rows, or the rows are filtered as part of the read operation. Therefore, as few rows as possible are input to the grouping operation, only the rows that is necessary for solving the task.

An expression in HAVING that filters on base data/table data is moved by the compiler to the WHERE clause before optimization. There cannot be an expression with an aggregation function in the WHERE clause because the value only exists after the grouping. Therefore, use WHERE and HAVING correctly! Not for optimization reasons, but for understanding and maintenance reasons. The compiler/optimizer corrects the optimization.

If the selection condition is written in HAVING the optimizer still create an optimal plan by moving this part from HAVING to be used when reading the data from the table. The optimizer saves time grouping on rows B and E to simply remove those rows later.

It is allowed to reference aggregation functions in HAVING which is not a column in the result table. The conditions learned in WHERE is allowed in HAVING. We can use =, >, <, BETWEEN, …

```
SELECT    Zipcode,
          COUNT (*)          AS Number
          FROM dbo.Person
          WHERE Zipcode BETWEEN 6000 AND 9000
          GROUP BY Zipcode
          HAVING COUNT (*) - COUNT (Zipcode) > 100;
```

In the following example Orders are extracted if the total Discount is greater than 10% of the total Amount for the Order. The table schema is

```
CREATE TABLE dbo.OrderLine
(
          OrderID         INT      NOT NULL,
          ProductID       INT      NOT NULL,
          Amount          INT      NOT NULL,
          Discount        INT      NULL,

          CONSTRAINT PK_OrderLine PRIMARY KEY (OrderID, ProductID)
);
```

We insert the following data.

```
INSERT INTO dbo.OrderLine (OrderID, ProductID, Amount, Discount) VALUES
          (1, 10, 1000, NULL),      (1, 22, 800, 25),     (1, 15, 4000, 600),    (1, 31, 300, 75),
          (1, 29, 900, NULL),       (2, 33, 800, NULL),   (2, 87, 600, NULL),    (3, 66, 700, 40),
          (4, 55, 600, 70),         (5, 58, 400, 50),     (5, 17, 200, 25);
```

First, we calculate the total Amount and Discount for each Order to use it to assess whether the chosen solution is correct.

```
SELECT    OrderID,
          SUM (Amount),
          SUM (Discount)
          FROM dbo.OrderLine
          GROUP BY OrderID;
```

OrderID		
1	7000	700
2	1400	NULL
3	700	40
4	600	70
5	600	75

With GROUP BY we are looking at each Order. We do not return Amount and Discount but only the OrderID.

```
SELECT    OrderID
          FROM dbo.OrderLine
          GROUP BY OrderID
          HAVING SUM (Amount) * 0.1 <= SUM (Discount);
```

OrderID
1
4
5

For evaluating the result we change the statement to select the Orders where the Discount is less than 10% if the total Amount. Because we in the statement above compare with <=, we use >.

```
SELECT    OrderID
          FROM dbo.OrderLine
          GROUP BY OrderID
          HAVING SUM (Amount) * 0.1 > SUM (Discount);
```

OrderID
3

Because OrderID = 2 only have NULL in the Discount column, the SUM (Discount) is also NULL. When comparing with SUM (Amount) with <= or with > is always false. Therefore OrderID = 2 is not in any of the result sets. So the solution is not correct.

There are two solutions to this problem. We can change the result of SUM to 0 if the SUM is NULL. Or we can change a NULL Discount to 0 before calculating SUM.

```
SELECT    OrderID
          FROM dbo.OrderLine
          GROUP BY OrderID
          HAVING SUM (Amount) * 0.1 > COALESCE (SUM (Discount), 0);
```

```
SELECT    OrderID
          FROM dbo.OrderLine
          GROUP BY OrderID
          HAVING SUM (Amount) * 0.1 > SUM (COALESCE (Discount, 0));
```

When developing a solution like this, it is important to test for correctness, including evaluating the 'opposite' condition. If we have 100 orders, and the solution with '>' results in 23 rows/order, it should be tested whether using '<=' results in 77 rows. Perhaps the evaluation for correctness should show the aggregations used in HAVING in the result, but remove these columns before the statement is used in production. It is important to spend time on evaluation, because it can be difficult to see the problems.

PARTITION BY

In this chapter we look at a general use of PARTITION BY, as experience shows that even beginners to SQL will encounter this option if they maintain a system. Many details are omitted, as the purpose is only to gain a general understanding.

With GROUP BY we reduce the number of rows by grouping/collapsing many rows from the input into one row in the result table. We can add columns to the result using the aggregation functions. The most commonly used aggregation functions are COUNT, SUM and AVG, but there are others.

OrderID	ProductID	SalesAmount
1	10	20
1	5	40
1	8	100
2	3	30
2	7	90
3	5	50
3	7	150
3	11	200

GROUP BY →

OrderID	TotalAmount	NumberOfOL
1	160	3
2	120	2
3	400	3

With PARTITION BY we keep all rows from the input but add calculated columns to the result, columns calculated on all or some of the rows in the partition. We can use the same aggregation functions as for GROUP BY, but there are others when using PARTITION BY. These are the ranking functions ROW_NUMBER, DENSE_RANK, RANK, and NTILE. With LAG and LEAD we can access a row with a given offset relative to the current row.

OrderID	ProductID	SalesAmount
1	10	20
1	5	40
1	8	100
2	3	30
2	7	90
3	5	50
3	7	150
3	11	200

PARTITION BY →

OrderID	ProductID	SalesAmount	RowNumber	RollingSum
1	10	20	1	20
1	5	40	2	60
1	8	100	3	160
2	3	30	1	30
2	7	90	2	120
3	5	50	1	50
3	7	150	2	200
3	11	200	3	400

For showing examples we use the same data as used earlier in the book.

```
CREATE TABLE dbo.CustomerSale
(
        ID              INT       NOT NULL IDENTITY
                        CONSTRAINT PK_CustomerSale PRIMARY KEY,
        CustomerID      INT       NOT NULL,
        OrderID         INT       NOT NULL,
        OrderDate       DATE      NOT NULL,
        Amount          INT       NOT NULL,
        Discount        INT       NULL

        CONSTRAINT UQ_CustomerSale UNIQUE (CustomerID, OrderID)
);
```

ID	CustomerID	OrderID	OrderDate	Amount	Discount
1	1	234	2024-04-09	4900	400
2	1	811	2024-05-10	500	NULL
3	1	934	2024-06-03	650	NULL
4	1	1021	2024-07-18	350	NULL
5	1	1233	2024-10-28	1700	200
6	3	111	2024-05-11	300	30
7	3	674	2024-08-16	950	90
8	3	812	2024-10-21	750	60
9	8	48	2023-11-26	700	45
10	8	122	2024-08-31	150	NULL
11	8	588	2024-09-20	250	25
12	8	608	2024-11-23	100	5
13	9	47	2024-04-05	2	NULL
14	9	56	2024-04-08	1	NULL

We look at the result of the following statement where the ranking functions ROW_NUMBER, DENSE_RANK, RANK and NTILE are used. Each partition is a Customer/CustomerID, so we have four partitions in the table above, we have the yellow, the green, the red and the blue partition.

Rows in a table are unordered, so for each partition it is necessary to specify the sort order in order to perform the subsequent operations uniquely. For the first three partitions, the rows are sorted by Discount. We can ORDER BY more than one column and can also specify ascending/ASC or descending/DESC. ASC is the default.

For the NTILE ranking function it is shown, that the table is one partition as known from grouping if we use the aggregation functions and do not specify GROUP BY. It is the same principle when PARTITION BY is omitted.

```
SELECT    CustomerID,
          OrderID,
          Amount,
          Discount,
          ROW_NUMBER ()      OVER (PARTITION BY CustomerID ORDER BY Discount)      AS ROW_NUMBER,
          RANK ()            OVER (PARTITION BY CustomerID ORDER BY Discount)      AS RANK,
          DENSE_RANK ()      OVER (PARTITION BY CustomerID ORDER BY Discount)      AS DENSE_RANK,
          NTILE (3)          OVER (ORDER BY CustomerID, OrderID)                   AS NTILE
          FROM dbo.CustomerSale
          ORDER BY CustomerID, Discount;
```

CustomerID	OrderID	Amount	Discount	ROW_NUMBER	RANK	DENSE_RANK	NTILE
1	811	500	NULL	1	1	1	1
1	934	650	NULL	2	1	1	1
1	1021	350	NULL	3	1	1	1
1	1233	1700	200	4	4	2	1
1	234	4900	400	5	5	3	1
3	111	300	30	1	1	1	2
3	812	750	60	2	2	2	2
3	674	950	90	3	3	3	2
8	122	150	NULL	1	1	1	2
8	608	100	5	2	2	2	3
8	588	250	25	3	3	3	3
8	48	700	45	4	4	4	2
9	47	2	NULL	1	1	1	3
9	56	1	NULL	2	1	1	3

The rows in the result are sorted by CustomerID, Discount. When sorting rows, NULL comes first.

If we look at the column ROW_NUMBER we can see that the rows are number 1, 2, 3 , … according to the sort order. When we have a new partition we start over with 1.

We look at the partition CustomerID = 1. For RANK, the first three rows have Discount = NULL, and therefore have RANK = 1. The fourth row has RANK = 4, because we have three rows before in the sort order. The last row in the partition has RANK = 5, because we have four rows before in the sort order. As can be seen, RANK 2 and 3 do not exist for this partition. When we get to the next partition where CustomerID is 2, we start over with 1.

With DENSE_RANK, we have the value 1 for the first three rows in the partition with CustomerID = 1. But the fourth row has the value 2 – DENSE – because the last of the three rows before has the value 1. The last row in the partition has the value 3.

For NTILE, the table is one partition. We divide the rows into 3 groups. Because we have 14 rows, the groups contain 5, 5, and 4 rows.

Next we are looking at how to use windowing function and partitions together with the aggregate functions.

```
SELECT    CustomerID,
          OrderID,
          Amount,
          SUM (Amount)      OVER (PARTITION BY CustomerID ORDER BY Amount, OrderID )      AS RunningTotal
          FROM dbo.CustomerSale
          ORDER BY CustomerID, Amount;
```

We add the first column ROW_NUMBER in the result, where the partition is the table for being used for the subsequent comments.

ROW_NUMBER	CustomerID	OrderID	Amount	RunningTotal
1	1	1021	350	350
2	1	811	500	850
3	1	934	650	1500
4	1	1233	1700	3200
5	1	234	4900	8100
6	3	111	300	300
7	3	812	750	1050
8	3	674	950	2000
9	8	608	100	100
10	8	122	150	250
11	8	588	250	500
12	8	48	700	1200
13	9	56	1	1
14	9	47	2	3

In this statement we have both partitions and frames. When calculating, only the rows within the current frame are used. A frame cannot go beyond the partition boundary. When we look at row number 1, the frame is only row number 1. When calculating for row number 2, the frame contains rows number 1 and 2. Therefore, RunningTotal is 350 + 500 = 850, etc.

```sql
SELECT   CustomerID,
         OrderID,
         Amount,
         Discount,
         SUM (Amount)        OVER (PARTITION BY CustomerID ORDER BY Amount, OrderID ) AS RunningTotal,
         Amount * 100.0 / SUM (Amount)        OVER (PARTITION BY CustomerID
                            ORDER BY CustomerID ROWS BETWEEN UNBOUNDED PRECEDING AND UNBOUNDED FOLLOWING) AS Pct
         FROM dbo.CustomerSale
         WHERE CustomerID = 1
         ORDER BY CustomerID, Amount;
```

We only look at the partition CustomerID = 1. For each Order, we calculate the Order's percentage of the Customers total Amount. We change the frame on which the calculation is made to the entire partition – ROWS BETWEEN UNBOUNDED PRECEDING AND UNBOUNDED FOLLOWING. The SUM of the Amount for the partition is 8100 and 350 is 4.32% of this – 350 *100 / 8100.

Defining a frame other than the default frame has many more options. But this is not reviewed in this book.

ROW_NUMBER	CustomerID	OrderID	Amount	Discount	RunningTotal	Pct
1	1	1021	350	NULL	350	4.320987654320
2	1	811	500	NULL	850	6.172839506172
3	1	934	650	NULL	1500	8.024691358024
4	1	1233	1700	200	3200	20.987654320987
5	1	234	4900	400	8100	60.493827160493

The last example shows the use of LAG. Again, we only look at CustomerID = 1.

```sql
SELECT   CustomerID,
         OrderID,
         OrderDate,
         LAG (OrderDate, 1)    OVER (PARTITION BY CustomerID ORDER BY Orderdate)                                AS LastOrder,
         DATEDIFF (DAY, LAG (OrderDate, 1)        OVER (PARTITION BY CustomerID ORDER BY OrderDate), OrderDate)    AS DaysBetween
         FROM dbo.CustomerSale
         WHERE CustomerID = 1
         ORDER BY CustomerID, OrderDate;
```

CustomerID	OrderID	OrderDate	LastOrder	DaysBetween
1	234	2024-04-10	NULL	NULL
1	811	2024-05-11	2024-04-10	31
1	934	2024-06-04	2024-05-11	24
1	1021	2024-07-19	2024-06-04	45
1	1233	2024-10-29	2024-07-19	102

Because we are working with sorted data, it is relevant to designate one of the rows before – LAG – or one of the rows after – LEAD. In this statement, we find the largest OrderDate less than the current OrderDate. For the first row, we had no predecessor. In the example, LAG (OrderDate, 1) is used to find the largest predecessor. We can specify any number as long as it is within the partition. With LEAD, we find descendants.

ORDER BY

Data in a table is unordered. Although SQL Server can define a Clustered Index on a table, it is only a logical order. Since the result table is a table, it is also unordered unless ORDER BY is specified.

Data can be sorted by one or more columns. For each column it can be specified whether it should be in ascending/ASC or descending/DESC order.

The sort column is specified either by the column name, the alias name specified in the projection, the column position in the result table, or by an expression. In SQL Server, it is possible to sort on a column that is not included in the result table, but this only applies to simple constructs. If the statement contains a GROUP BY, this is – logically – not possible, since a single row in the result can be formed from multiple rows. These rows that are part of a group can have different values in the column that we want to sort by.

When sorting in ascending order on a column where one or more of the rows is NULL for the column being sorted on, the first rows after sorting will be NULL for the sorting column, regardless of the data type. Even though NULL is not a value, it still has a 'place/position' in the sort order. For other products, it can be specified whether NULL should come first or last, but not in SQL Server. We have to handle this ourselves.

We use the following data.

```
CREATE TABLE dbo.Zipinfo
(
        Zipcode              SMALLINT           NOT NULL
                             CONSTRAINT PK_Zipinfo PRIMARY KEY,
        City                 VARCHAR (20)       NOT NULL
);


CREATE TABLE dbo.CustomerType
(
        CustomerTypeID       CHAR (1)           NOT NULL
                             CONSTRAINT PK_CustomerType PRIMARY KEY,
        CustomerTypeTxt      VARCHAR (20)       NOT NULL
                             CONSTRAINT UQ_CustomerType_CustomerTypeTxt UNIQUE
);


CREATE TABLE dbo.Customer
(
        CustomerID           INT                NOT NULL
                             CONSTRAINT PK_Customer PRIMARY KEY,
        Name                 VARCHAR (35)       NOT NULL,
        Address              VARCHAR (35)       NULL,
        Zipcode              SMALLINT           NULL
                             CONSTRAINT FK_Customer_Zipinfo FOREIGN KEY REFERENCES dbo.Zipinfo (Zipcode),
        CustomerTypeID       CHAR (1)           NULL
                             CONSTRAINT FK_Customer_CustomerType FOREIGN KEY REFERENCES dbo.CustomerType (CustomerTypeID),
);
GO
INSERT INTO dbo.Zipinfo (Zipcode, City) VALUES
        (2000, 'Frederiksberg'),      (5000, 'Odense'),        (8000, 'Aarhus C'),        (9000, 'Aalborg');

INSERT INTO dbo.CustomerType (CustomerTypeID, CustomerTypeTxt) VALUES
        ('C', 'Company'),             ('O', 'Ordinary'),       ('P', 'Public');

INSERT INTO dbo.Customer (CustomerID, Name, Address, Zipcode, CustomerTypeID) VALUES
        (1, 'John Olsson', 'Nygade 22', 2000, 'O'),           (2, 'Ane Anderson', NULL, NULL, NULL),
        (3, 'Company1', NULL, NULL, 'C'),                     (4, 'Peter Poulsen', 'Vestergade 34', 8000, NULL),
        (5, 'Peter Poulsen', NULL, NULL, 'O'),                (6, 'Irene Knudsen', 'Torvet 13', 8000, 'O');
```

In the first statement the sort order is by the columns Name and Address.

```
SELECT    *
        FROM dbo.Customer
        ORDER BY Name, Address;
```

CustomerID	Name	Address	Zipcode	CustomerTypeID
2	Ane Anderson	NULL	NULL	NULL
3	Company1	NULL	NULL	C
6	Irene Knudsen	Torvet 13	8000	O
1	John Olsson	Nygade 22	2000	O
5	Peter Poulsen	NULL	NULL	O
4	Peter Poulsen	Vestergade 34	8000	NULL

We have two rows with the Name 'Peter Poulsen'. CustomerID = 5 comes before CustomerID = 4 because the address is NULL for CustomerID = 5.

In the next example, the column number is used. The column number is the number in the result table. Column numbers should never be used in production, as it makes the statement less readable and maintenance errors can occur if a new column is inserted into the result. The result is the same as for the above statement.

```
SELECT    *
          FROM dbo.Customer
          ORDER BY 2, 3;
```

In the next example, a column that is not included in the results table is the sort order column.

```
SELECT    CustomerID,
          Name
          FROM dbo.Customer
          ORDER BY Zipcode;
```

CustomerID	Name
2	Ane Anderson
3	Company1
5	Peter Poulsen
1	John Olsson
6	Irene Knudsen
4	Peter Poulsen

Both CustomerID 2, 3 and 5 have NULL in the Zipcode column.

If we want Customers with NULL in the column Zipcode to come last in the sort order, we can use one of the following statements. When using a constant the data type must be known to be sure that the value is bigger than all values in the table now and in the future.

The Sub-Select as parameter in the COALESCE function in the second statement is explained in the next chapter. If we select the largest Zipcode value and add one to that number, rows with NULL will come last. We add 1 because the column has a numeric data type. It is important for this example that NULL still appears in the result. Be careful not to return fake/non-existent data just because you use this data for sorting.

```
SELECT    CustomerID,
          Name,
          Zipcode
          FROM dbo.Customer
          ORDER BY COALESCE (Zipcode, 9999);
```

```
SELECT    CustomerID,
          Name,
          Zipcode
          FROM dbo.Customer
          ORDER BY COALESCE (Zipcode, (SELECT MAX (Zipcode) + 1 FROM dbo.Zipinfo));
```

CustomerID	Name	Zipcode
1	John Olsson	2000
4	Peter Poulsen	8000
6	Irene Knudsen	8000
5	Peter Poulsen	NULL
2	Ane Anderson	NULL
3	Company1	NULL

If we want to use the same principle for the CustomerType column, we can't add 1 because the column has the data type CHAR(1). However, we can use a column with a data type accepting more characters by using the COALESCE function. If we use ISNULL instead of COALESCE, the data type will not change, but the value will simply be shortened to CHAR(1). We show NULL in the result table but order by another value – in the example 'PX' instead of NULL because MAX (CustomerType) is 'P'.

We could select the MAX (CustomerTypeID) from the table dbo.Customer, but for this example it will give the same result because the FOREIGN KEY is defined. The NULL when sorting will instead be 'OX' but it do not matter because 'OX' is larger than all the CustomerTypeID in the table dbo.Customer.

```
SELECT    CustomerID,
          Name,
          CustomerTypeID
          FROM dbo.Customer
          ORDER BY COALESCE (CustomerTypeID, (SELECT COALESCE (MAX (CustomerTypeID), 'X') FROM dbo.CustomerType));
```

CustomerID	Name	CustomerTypeID
3	Company1	C
1	John Olsson	O
5	Peter Poulsen	O
6	Irene Knudsen	O
2	Ane Anderson	NULL
4	Peter Poulsen	NULL

Sub-Select

A Sub-Select is a SELECT statement that is part of another DML statement. Since a SELECT statement returns a table, a Sub-Select will also return a table. But it is important to focus on the schema of the table returned from a Sub-Select. If we use a Sub-Select in the Projection of a SELECT statement, it must be possible to convert the result to a value. Therefore, the schema of the return table must be one column. The number of rows must be 0 or 1. If we use a Sub-Select in FROM, the return table can have many columns and many rows, as we know from all the other tables used in FROM. In WHERE, it depends on which expression we specify. For a comparison, there are the same restrictions as for a Sub-Select in the Projection, because we can only compare with one value. If it is the value list for the IN operator, there must be only one column, but many rows. For EXISTS, it must be a table with an arbitrary structure and number of rows.

In the following, some examples are shown and some issues are discussed. We use the same tables and data as above.

```sql
CREATE TABLE dbo.Zipinfo
(
        Zipcode              SMALLINT          NOT NULL
                             CONSTRAINT PK_Zipinfo PRIMARY KEY,
        City                 VARCHAR (20)      NOT NULL
);

CREATE TABLE dbo.CustomerType
(
        CustomerTypeID       CHAR (1)          NOT NULL
                             CONSTRAINT PK_CustomerType PRIMARY KEY,
        CustomerTypeTxt      VARCHAR (20)      NOT NULL
                             CONSTRAINT UQ_CustomerType_CustomerTypeTxt UNIQUE
);

CREATE TABLE dbo.Customer
(
        CustomerID           INT               NOT NULL
                             CONSTRAINT PK_Customer PRIMARY KEY,
        Name                 VARCHAR (35)      NOT NULL,
        Address              VARCHAR (35)      NULL,
        Zipcode              SMALLINT          NULL
                             CONSTRAINT FK_Customer_Zipinfo FOREIGN KEY REFERENCES dbo.Zipinfo (Zipcode),
        CustomerTypeID       CHAR (1)          NOT NULL
                             CONSTRAINT FK_Customer_CustomerType FOREIGN KEY REFERENCES dbo.CustomerType (CustomerTypeID),
);

CREATE TABLE dbo.CustomerSale
(
        ID                   INT               NOT NULL          IDENTITY
                             CONSTRAINT PK_CustomerSale PRIMARY KEY,
        CustomerID           INT               NOT NULL,
        OrderID              INT               NOT NULL,
        OrderDate            DATE              NOT NULL,
        Amount               INT               NOT NULL,
        Discount             INT               NULL

        CONSTRAINT UQ_CustomerSale UNIQUE (CustomerID, OrderID)
);
GO
INSERT INTO dbo.Zipinfo (Zipcode, City) VALUES
        (2000, 'Frederiksberg'),        (5000, 'Odense'),        (8000, 'Aarhus C'),        (9000, 'Aalborg');

INSERT INTO dbo.CustomerType (CustomerTypeID, CustomerTypeTxt) VALUES
        ('C', 'Company'),        ('O', 'Ordinary'),        ('P', 'Public');

INSERT INTO dbo.Customer (CustomerID, Name, Address, Zipcode, CustomerTypeID) VALUES
        (1, 'John Olsson', 'Nygade 22', 2000, 'O'),        (2, 'Ane Anderson', NULL, NULL, NULL),
        (3, 'Company1', NULL, NULL, 'C'),        (4, 'Peter Poulsen', 'Vestergade 34', 8000, NULL),
        (5, 'Peter Poulsen', NULL, NULL, 'O'),        (6, 'Irene Knudsen', 'Torvet 13', 8000, 'O');
INSERT INTO dbo.CustomerSale (CustomerID, OrderID, OrderDate, Amount, Discount) VALUES
```

```
(1, 234, DATEADD (DAY, -230, SYSDATETIME ()), 4900, 400),        (1, 811, DATEADD (DAY, -199, SYSDATETIME ()), 500, NULL),
(1, 934, DATEADD (DAY, -175, SYSDATETIME ()), 650, NULL),        (1, 1021, DATEADD (DAY, -130, SYSDATETIME ()), 350, NULL),
(1, 1233, DATEADD (DAY, -28, SYSDATETIME ()), 1700, 200),

(3, 111, DATEADD (DAY, -198, SYSDATETIME ()), 300, 30),          (3, 674, DATEADD (DAY, -101, SYSDATETIME ()), 950, 90),
(3, 812, DATEADD (DAY, -35, SYSDATETIME ()), 750, 60),

(4, 48, DATEADD (DAY, -365, SYSDATETIME ()), 700, 45),           (4, 122, DATEADD (DAY, -86, SYSDATETIME ()), 150, NULL),
(4, 588, DATEADD (DAY, -66, SYSDATETIME ()), 250, 25),           (4, 608, DATEADD (DAY, -2, SYSDATETIME ()), 100, 5),

(6, 47, DATEADD (DAY, -234, SYSDATETIME ()), 2, NULL),           (6, 56, DATEADD (DAY, -231, SYSDATETIME ()), 1, NULL);
```

In the first statement, a Sub-Select is used in FROM. The Sub-Select below returns the following table where the number of Customers are count for each Zipcode value.

Zipcode	NumberCust
NULL	3
2000	1
8000	2

In the statement, we join this intermediate result from the Sub-Select named CustAgg with the dbo.Customer table – a simple join between two tables. Since there are Customers where the Zipcode column is NULL, a RIGHT JOIN is specified for showing that we have 3 Customers without a Zipcode value. If this information is not to be included in the result, an INNER JOIN is performed instead.

```
SELECT      *
       FROM dbo.Zipinfo RIGHT JOIN (SELECT      Zipcode,
                                           COUNT (*)            AS NumberCust
                                    FROM dbo.Customer
                                    GROUP BY Zipcode)           AS CustAgg
       ON Zipinfo.Zipcode = CustAgg.Zipcode;
```

Zipcode	City	Zipcode	NumberCust
NULL	NULL	NULL	3
2000	Frederiksberg	2000	1
8000	Aarhus C	8000	2

If we instead use a Sub-Select in the Projection, we cannot include Customers with NULL in Zipcode, but we have all Zipcodes from the dbo.Zipinfo table included in the result. The Sub-Select used returns a table with one column and one row. This cell can implicitly be converted to a value. If we have a Zipcode in dbo.Zipinfo without a related Customer in the dbo.Customer table, the aggregation function COUNT (*) in the Sub-Select returns 0. One column and one row is a requirement for the result from a Sub-Select in the Projection to be converted to a value. If the Sub-Select returns one column but no rows, the result is converted to NULL.

```
SELECT      *,
       (SELECT      COUNT (*)            AS NumberCust
               FROM dbo.Customer
               WHERE Customer.Zipcode = Zipinfo.Zipcode)        AS NumberCust
       FROM dbo.Zipinfo;
```

Zipcode	City	
2000	Frederiksberg	1
5000	Odense	0
8000	Aarhus C	2
9000	Aalborg	0

If we change the first statement from RIGHT to FULL JOIN, there will be 5 rows in the results table The 4 green rows from dbo.Zipinfo table and the yellow row that tells that there are 3 Customers without a Zipcode. But because of FULL JOIN the column NumberCust is NULL for the Zipcode in dbo.Zipinfo without related rows in dbo.Customer. This shows that we must decide which solution to use in a task like this.

```sql
SELECT      *
       FROM dbo.Zipinfo FULL JOIN (SELECT          Zipcode,
                                          COUNT (*)           AS NumberCust
                            FROM dbo.Customer
                            GROUP BY Zipcode)          AS CustAgg
                      ON Zipinfo.Zipcode = CustAgg.Zipcode;
```

Zipcode	City	Zipcode	NumberCust
NULL	NULL	NULL	3
2000	Frederiksberg	2000	1
5000	Odense	NULL	NULL
8000	Aarhus C	8000	2
9000	Aalborg	NULL	NULL

The Sub-Select that appears in the Projection is a correlated Sub-Select. This means that the calculation in the Sub-Select is linked to a row in the outer table with the condition Customer.Zipcode = Zipinfo.Zipcode. Semantically, the Sub-Select must be executed as many times as there are rows in the outer table, but SQL Server optimizes this at compile time.

The Sub-Select specified in FROM is executed once and produces an intermediate result which is a table. This intermediate result is joined with the other table specified in FROM. Nothing special, just a join between two tables where we have to decide the join condition and the join type. The two tables in FROM could be two intermediate results from two Sub-Selects.

When using a Sub-Select in WHERE or HAVING it is different how the result table should look like.

Column = (Sub-Select)	The comparation operator can be =. <, >, <=, >= or <>. The result must return one column and zero or on row
Column IN (Sub-Select)	The result must return one column but many rows.
Column BETWEEN (Sub-Select1) AND (Sub-Select2)	Both Sub-Select must return one column and zero or one row.
EXISTS (Sub-Select)	The Sub-Select must return any table structure.

In the first example, it is a simple comparison. We want to select CustomerSale rows where the Amount is greater than the average of all the CustomerSale rows. The average for all CustomerSale is 807.

```sql
SELECT      *
       FROM dbo.CustomerSale
       WHERE Amount > (SELECT AVG (Amount) FROM dbo.CustomerSale);
```

ID	CustomerID	OrderID	OrderDate	Amount	Discount
1	1	234	2024-04-11	4900	400
5	1	1233	2024-10-30	1700	200
7	3	674	2024-08-18	950	90

The next Sub-Select returns Customers who have received more than 10% discount in the last 3 months.

```sql
SELECT      *
       FROM dbo.Customer
       WHERE CustomerID IN (SELECT CustomerID
                     FROM dbo.CustomerSale
                     WHERE    Amount * 0.1 < Discount        AND
                              OrderDate > DATEADD (MONTH, -3, SYSDATETIME ()));
```

CustomerID	Name	Address	Zipcode	CustomerTypeID
1	John Olsson	Nygade 22	2000	O

In the next example, we check if an Order EXISTS for a Customer where the OrderDate value is less than 6 months old. These Customers are returned. The expression is true – returns the Customer – if the Sub-Select statement returns at least one row. In the Sub-Select, * is specified in the Projection. In SQL Server, it does not give better performance if a column or a constant is specified instead. Even NULL is seen as the Projection data in a Sub-Select. The compiler find the best way to solve the problem. The argument for not specifying * is that with an asterisk the row is read. But the optimizer may be able to solve the problem by seeking in an index. Therefore, * is specified.

```sql
SELECT *
    FROM dbo.Customer
    WHERE EXISTS (SELECT          *
        FROM dbo.CustomerSale
        WHERE   CustomerSale.CustomerID = Customer.CustomerID        AND
                CustomerSale.OrderDate > DATEADD(MONTH, -6, SYSDATETIME ()));
```

CustomerID	Name	Address	Zipcode	CustomerTypeID
1	John Olsson	Nygade 22	2000	O
3	Company1	NULL	NULL	C
4	Peter Poulsen	Vestergade 34	8000	NULL

In a company we don't follow the calendar month, but have a table that shows how the months are defined. In our own calendar a month always start at a Sunday. This is sometimes used for having comparable month where the number of working days/opening days are the same number. This table is defined with the columns Year, Month, StartDate, and EndDate.

Year	Month	StartDate	EndDate
…	…	…	…
2024	August	2024-8-4	2024-8-31
2024	September	2024-9-1	2024-9-29
…	…	…	…

If we want to SELECT all the CustomerSale data from September 2024, we use the following statement with BETWEEN and two Sub-Select.

```sql
SELECT      *
    FROM dbo.CustomerSale
    WHERE OrderDate BETWEEN    (SELECT    StartDate
                                FROM dbo.Calendar
                                WHERE Year = 2024 AND Month = 'September')      AND
                               (SELECT    EndDate
                                FROM dbo.Calendar
                                WHERE Year = 2024 AND Month = 'September');
```

It is not maintainable to have statements that are too static and therefore need to be fixed frequently. Therefore, Sub-Select should be used and values stored in or calculated from rows in a table. In the last example above, the current month could perhaps be calculated from SYSDATETIME ().

On the internet we come across many discussions about whether it is better to use IN instead of EXISTS. Maybe join perform better? Of course, it depends on the database product that we are using. But for the following 4 statements exactly the same execution plan is formed in SQL Server. When these claims are made, it is important to be aware of whether this also applies to the database system you are using. There may be a difference. In the third statement, DISTINCT is included in the Sub-Select. The argument may be that it must be faster if the Sub-Select returns fewer CustomerID values. But all four statements are 'translated' to an INNER JOIN in SQL Server, so it does not help to try all possible more or less undocumented optimization suggestions. Use the construction that you find most understandable or that is the company standard.

```sql
SELECT      DISTINCT Customer.*
    FROM dbo.Customer INNER JOIN dbo.CustomerSale ON Customer.CustomerID = CustomerSale.CustomerID;


SELECT      Customer.*
    FROM dbo.Customer
    WHERE CustomerID IN (SELECT    CustomerID
                         FROM dbo.CustomerSale);


SELECT      Customer.*
    FROM dbo.Customer
    WHERE CustomerID IN (SELECT    DISTINCT CustomerID
                         FROM dbo.CustomerSale);
```

```sql
SELECT     Customer.*
    FROM dbo.Customer
    WHERE EXISTS (SELECT          CustomerID
                      FROM dbo.CustomerSale
                      WHERE Customer.CustomerID = CustomerSale.CustomerID);
```

The next chapter about Views introduces the use of CTE as an alternative. CTE can also serve as an alternative to Sub-Select to make a statement more readable and maintainable.

View

A View is a SELECT statement that is stored in the system tables. The text/statement for a view is 'mixed' with the statement that refers to the view before compilation and optimization. Therefore, it is not necessary to complicate the concepts by calling a view a virtual table. If a view joins 3 tables but only columns from two of the tables are referenced when used, the compiler/optimizer can in some situations ignore one of the tables. This is called join elimination. This topic is not discussed further in this book, but is among other things the reason why the term virtual table is misleading. A view is just a stored text containing one SELECT statement.

It is possible in SQL Server to persist the result from executing the view. This possibility is called a 'materialized view' in Oracle which is a more descriptive name than an 'indexed view' as being called in SQL Server. Persisted tables are in SQL Server stored as a Heap or as a Clustered Index. A persisted view must always be stored as a Clustered Index and surely the reason for the name. When we SELECT rows we do not care about how data is stored - it is only interesting when we talk about performance, not when we talk about how to write a query for a correct result. When we use a view, the statement still works if we switch from a persisted view to a non-persisted view or vice versa. When the base tables referenced in the view are updated, the data in the persisted view's Clustered Index is updated as part of the transaction.

Why use views? Maybe users need data from different tables. The tables must be joined, and even with different join types and perhaps with an advanced join condition. Since the data types and formulas used require calculations to be written in a certain way, it can be an advantage to define the extract as a view. We have seen earlier in the book that percent calculation can give different results depending on whether we write Amount / 100 * Percent or the formula is written as Amount * Percent / 100. By using a view, we are sure that everyone gets data according to the same principles/rules. Not necessary the correct result, but the same result. If it is found that the view's result is not correct, the view can be changed and everyone who uses the view will now get the new, same result. We use the same tables than used in earlier chapters.

```sql
CREATE TABLE dbo.Zipinfo                                    CREATE TABLE dbo.CustomerType
(                                                           (
    Zipcode    SMALLINT          NOT NULL                       CustomerTypeID    CHAR (1)          NOT NULL
               CONSTRAINT PK_Zipinfo PRIMARY KEY,                                 CONSTRAINT PK_CustomerType PRIMARY KEY,
    City       VARCHAR (20)      NOT NULL                       CustomerTypeTxt   VARCHAR (20)      NOT NULL
);                                                                                CONSTRAINT UQ_CustomerType_Txt UNIQUE
                                                            );
```

```sql
CREATE TABLE dbo.Customer
(
    CustomerID        INT            NOT NULL
                      CONSTRAINT PK_Customer PRIMARY KEY,
    Name              VARCHAR (35)   NOT NULL,
    Address           VARCHAR (35)   NULL,
    Zipcode           SMALLINT       NULL
                      CONSTRAINT FK_Customer_Zipinfo FOREIGN KEY REFERENCES dbo.Zipinfo (Zipcode),
    CustomerTypeID    CHAR (1)       NOT NULL
                      CONSTRAINT FK_Customer_CustomerType FOREIGN KEY REFERENCES dbo.CustomerType (CustomerTypeID),
);
```

```sql
CREATE TABLE dbo.CustomerSale
(
    ID            INT            NOT NULL              IDENTITY
                  CONSTRAINT PK_CustomerSale PRIMARY KEY,
    CustomerID    INT            NOT NULL,
```

```
    OrderID              INT              NOT NULL,
    OrderDate            DATE             NOT NULL,
    Amount               INT              NOT NULL,
    Discount             INT              NULL
    CONSTRAINT UQ_CustomerSale UNIQUE (CustomerID, OrderID)
);
```

If we look at the table definitions above, we can see that a Customer does not necessarily have data about Address and Zipcode. A user of the data believes that all Customers must have an Address and Zipcode. Giving the user read permissions to the view but not to the base tables, we ensure that a LEFT JOIN is used instead of an INNER JOIN. The join with the dbo.CustomerType table is an INNER JOIN because all Customers have a CustomerType value. If the Customer table have many columns some of this columns can be left out in the view.

```
CREATE VIEW dbo.CustomerData
AS
SELECT     Customer.CustomerID,
           Customer.Name,
           Customer.Address,
           Customer.Zipcode,
           Zipinfo.City,
           CustomerType.CustomerTypeTxt
           FROM dbo.Customer  INNER JOIN dbo.CustomerType  ON Customer.CustomerTypeID= CustomerType.CustomerTypeID
                              LEFT JOIN dbo.Zipinfo        ON Customer.Zipcode = Zipinfo.Zipcode;
```

To show what can happen when the view is referenced, we execute the following two SELECT statements. The first statement selects all columns from the view. The second statement selects only the columns that come from the base tables dbo.Customer and dbo.Zipinfo.

```
SELECT     *
           FROM dbo.CustomerData;

SELECT     CustomerID,
           Name,
           Address,
           Zipcode,
           City
           FROM dbo.CustomerData;
```

Without going into details, we can see in the graphical execution plan that the dbo.CustomerType table is ignored for the second statement. This proves that it is important to select only the columns that need to be used. We can also see that the base tables are referenced and the view name is not shown in the plan. Therefore, no virtual table. This elimination of a table also change the execution time. The estimated time is 60% and 40% of the total time. But the most important thing is that by using the view, the correct join type is used when selecting Customers.

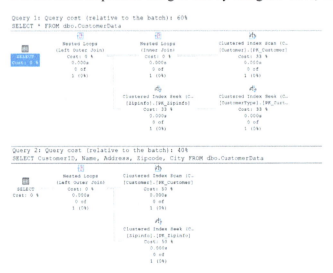

For the next view we only returns Ordinary Customers and not Companies and Public Customers. There is a rule in the company that some users are only allowed to see Customers in this category.

```sql
-- Only Ordinary Customers
CREATE VIEW dbo.OrdinaryCustomer
AS
SELECT     Customer.CustomerID,
           Customer.Name,
           Customer.Address,
           Customer.Zipcode,
           Zipinfo.City
           FROM dbo.Customer  LEFT JOIN dbo.Zipinfo            ON Customer.Zipcode = Zipinfo.Zipcode
           WHERE Customer.CustomerTypeID = 'O';
```

The last view returns the total Order amount for customers, but only for Orders from the last year. We use INNER JOIN to exclude Customers who have not made a purchase within the last year.

```sql
-- CustomerSale last year
CREATE VIEW dbo.CustomerSaleLastYear
AS
SELECT     Customer.CustomerID,
           Customer.Name,
           Customer.Address,
           Customer.Zipcode,
           Zipinfo.City,
           CustSale.AmountLastYear
           FROM dbo.Customer  LEFT JOIN dbo.Zipinfo ON Customer.Zipcode = Zipinfo.Zipcode
                         INNER JOIN (SELECT   CustomerSale.CustomerID,
                                     SUM (CustomerSale.Amount)           AS AmountLastYear
                                     FROM dbo.CustomerSale
                                     WHERE CustomerSale.OrderDate < DATEADD (YEAR, -1, SYSDATETIME ())
                                     GROUP BY CustomerSale.CustomerID)          AS CustSale
                     ON Customer.CustomerID = CustSale.CustomerID;
```

When a view is created, all columns must have a unique name that matches the syntax rules for a table. In some views, columns may have a different name because the column name in the database is 'bad'. It is not necessary to give the column an alias name in the SELECT statement, as the column can be named in the CREATE VIEW statement.

```sql
CREATE VIEW dbo.CustomerSaleLastYear (CustumerNumber, CustomerName, ....)
```

Views are sometimes defined for the purpose of being able to write the statement. This could be the case with the above view dbo.CustomerSaleLastYear. If we develop systems in this way, we can easily end up with a database with many views and no one can really get an overview of which views can be reused or which ones need to be fixed when changing the database.

If a view cannot be reused, it may be beneficial to use a CTE instead of. CTE stands for CommonTableExpression. With CTE, a SELECT statement is defined and named similar to a view. The CTE definition can only be used in the statement in which it is defined. In principle, it is to name a Sub-Select at the beginning of the statement. A CTE cannot be defined without a subsequent manipulation statement.

The following is three different ways of creating a solution to a task. The first statement use a Sub-Select in the middle of the statement. Think about the clarity and readability if we have four Sub-Select statements.

```sql
SELECT     Customer.CustomerID,
           Customer.Name,
           CustSale.SumAmount,
           CustSale.AvgAmount,
           CustSale.MinAmount,
           CustSale.MaxAmount
```

```
FROM dbo.Customer INNER JOIN (SELECT    CustomerSale.CustomerID,
                                        SUM (CustomerSale.Amount)    AS SumAmount,
                                        AVG (CustomerSale.Amount)    AS AvgAmount,
                                        MIN (CustomerSale.Amount)    AS MinAmount,
                                        MAX (CustomerSale.Amount)    AS MaxAmount
                                        FROM dbo.CustomerSale
                                        GROUP BY CustomerSale.CustomerID)    AS CustSale
                        ON Customer.CustomerID = CustSale.CustomerID;
```

For the next statement, we use a CTE. A CTE is simply a named definition at the beginning of a statement and is then used in the SELECT statement. For me, this statement is more readable and understandable.

```
WITH CustSale
AS
(
SELECT     CustomerSale.CustomerID,
           SUM (CustomerSale.Amount)    AS SumAmount,
           AVG (CustomerSale.Amount)    AS AvgAmount,
           MIN (CustomerSale.Amount)    AS MinAmount,
           MAX (CustomerSale.Amount)    AS MaxAmount
           FROM dbo.CustomerSale
           GROUP BY CustomerSale.CustomerID
)
SELECT     Customer.CustomerID,
           Customer.Name,
           CustSale.SumAmount,
           CustSale.AvgAmount,
           CustSale.MinAmount,
           CustSale.MaxAmount
           FROM dbo.Customer INNER JOIN CustSale ON Customer.CustomerID = CustSale.CustomerID;
```

Multiple CTE statements can be defined in the same statement. If there are many Sub-Selects in a statement, it is preferable in terms of understanding and in terms of readability to use CTE.

The last example show a join of the view dbo.CustomerData and a CTE. From the view only some of the columns are chosen and we use a CTE to aggregate CustomerSale. In this way the right join types are used for dbo.CustomerData and we have a statement that is simple and easy to overview because we only are joining two tables with INNER JOIN.

```
WITH
SalesData
AS
(
SELECT     CustomerSale.CustomerID,
           SUM (CustomerSale.Amount)    AS SumAmount,
           AVG (CustomerSale.Amount)    AS AvgAmount,
           MIN (CustomerSale.Amount)    AS MinAmount,
           MAX (CustomerSale.Amount)    AS MaxAmount
           FROM dbo.CustomerSale
           GROUP BY CustomerSale.CustomerID
)
SELECT     CustomerData.CustomerID,
           CustomerData.Name,
           CustomerData.City,
           SalesData.SumAmount,
           SalesData.AvgAmount,
           SalesData.MinAmount,
           SalesData.MaxAmount
           FROM dbo.CustomerData INNER JOIN SalesData ON CustomerData.CustomerID = SalesData.CustomerID;
```

Looking at this example it will be easy to develop a statement that are grouping the SalesData by the Customer-Type value.

Index

This chapter on indexes is not intended to teach you how to define indexes. This topic is large and complex. You should not just define many indexes for a database/table, as this will cause more problems than you are trying to solve. You should define indexes that can be used by many queries, not an index for a single or few queries. The purpose is to understand what can be read from an execution plan.

In this chapter we introduce Clustered and NonClustered Index. It is important to point out that a Clustered Index stores data in logical order. One of the worst myths about Clustered Indexes claims that data is sorted when a new row is inserted or a row is updated because the data is stored in physical order. Simple logic tells us that this is wrong! If a row is inserted in a table with several million rows, the insertion will take so long time that the product is useless if the rows are sorted first. Try to consider whether a claim can actually work in reality. This can help dispel some of the worst myths.

The following sketch shows how a Clustered Index are stored. The Clustered Index is a table where the data is logical ordered. If no order exist the table is stored as a HEAP. A database is stored in files, where each file is divided into extents - 64KB blocks. An extent is divided into 8 physical contiguous pages of 8KB each. In the sketch, the PRIMARY KEY is the ID column.

On a page, the rows are ordered by the ClusterKey/ID value. In the sketch, the ClusterKey is a numeric value. Each row use about 1800 bytes of data - Firstname, Lastname, Address, ..., so 4 rows can be stored on each page. We have pointers to the NextPage and to the PrevPage in the logical order. We look at the following file that stores data in a Clustered Index. The table use extents 5, 6 and 9. The other extents are used for other objects such as other tables or indexes or are still unused. In the sketch only the ID value is shown.

We can Scan the table which means that all rows are read. But for better performance we can Seek in the table which means that only some of the rows are read.

What happens when we Scan the table.

- From the system table sys.indexes we know, that the tables first row are on page 34.
- From this page we read the rows with ID value 1, 2, 4 and 6.
- Then we read page 37, the NextPage in ID logical order after page 34.
- From this page we then read the ID values 8, 9, and 10.
- The NextPage is page 66.
- Where we get data about ID value 13, 14 and 17.
- We read then the next page which is page 32.
- On this page we have the ID values 19 and 23.
- Next page is page 47.
- From this page we get the ID values 24, 28 and 30.
- Because the pointer to the next page is NULL we have finished scanning the table.
- The result from the operation is the ID values 1, 2, 4, 6, 8, 9, 10, 13, 14, 17, 19, 23, 24, 28 and 30. All the data is read in ID value order.

	Extent 5							
Page_id	32	33	34	35	36	37	38	39
Previous Page	66		Null			34		
Next Page	47		37			66		
Data	19, 23		1, 2, 4, 6			8, 9, 10		

	Extent 6							
Page_id	40	41	42	43	44	45	46	47
Previous Page								32
Next Page								Null
Data								24, 28, 30

	Extent 9							
Page_id	64	65	66	67	68	69	70	71
Previous Page			32					
Next Page			37					
Data			13, 14, 17					

It is important that the rows are only guaranteed to be ordered if ORDER BY is specified in the statement. SQL Server can choose to read data in page order by using the IAM page and can therefore return the rows in the following order. The pages in the file that contains data about this table in numeric order is 32, 34, 37, 47 and 66.

19, 23, 1, 2, 4, 6, 8, 9, 10, 24, 28, 30, 13, 14, 17

If the compiler chooses to read data in parallel, the order will be different and unknown.

For Scanning the table we read data from 5 pages. This pages are stored in 3 extents. An extent are often the block that is read/loaded into memory. If we REBUILD the index we could have all the data stored in one extent on 4 pages and even 4 empty pages allocated for new rows in the table, because the extent is allocated to the table.

If we INSERT a row with the ID value 21, the row must be stored on page 32 to keep the data in logical order. No problem, because there are only 2 rows on the page and we can store up to 4 rows on each page.

	Extent 5							
Page_id	32	33	34	35	36	37	38	39
Previous Page	66		Null			34		
Next Page	47		37			66		
Data	19, 21, 23		1, 2, 4, 6			8, 9, 10		

If we INSERT a row with the ID value 5, we have a problem. The row must be stored on page 34, where 4 rows are already stored. A page split is performed where half of the rows are moved to a new page. We have empty pages in the same extent that can be used. If not, the system must find an empty page in a different extent somewhere else in the file or perhaps even in a different file if the database is created with multiple data files.

Page 34 is split by moving half of the rows to page 35. The NextPage and PrevPage pointers are updated.

	Extent 5							
Page_id	32	33	34	35	36	37	38	39
Previous Page	66		Null	34		35		
Next Page	47		35	37		66		
Data	19, 21, 23		1, 2,	4, 6		8, 9, 10		

The new row with ID value 5 can now be inserted on one of the 2 pages depending on the ID value. For this example, the row will be inserted on page 35

	Extent 5							
Page_id	32	33	34	35	36	37	38	39
Previous Page	66		Null	34		35		
Next Page	47		35	37		66		
Data	19, 21, 23		1, 2,	4, 5, 6		8, 9, 10		

All rows are still in logical order and can be read in that order if desired, as shown above. This is a choice of the optimizer/compiler. This example shows how data in a table becomes fragmented. We don't care about this when we write a query, but the DBA might decide to rebuild or reorganize the table.

The Clustered Index also have a root page, that is used when we want to select one or an interval of ID values. The Index pages contains a reference to the lowest ID value on each page together with the page on which this value is stored. The values shown are after INSERT of ID value 21 and 5. The reference is file_id:page_id. If we are Seeking for ID value 7 we can see from the Index root page that if the ID value is stored in the table, the row must be found on page 1:35. On this page the lowest value is 4 and the lowest value on the next page is 8. If we search for the ID value 6, the exact same action must be performed. ID = 7 is not found in the table, but ID = 6 is found in the table. We read page 1:35 and look for the existents of the value.

Min value on the page	Page_id
1	1:34
4	1:35
8	1:37
13	1:66
24	1:47

If we want the rows in the range of ID values from 5 to 20, we can start with a Seek operation on the value 5 and then continue with Scan of the table. The Scan operation stops when we read a value greater than 20.

For a small table like this, we only have one Index page/the root page for the Clustered Index containing 5 rows. It could be many pages organized in a hierarchy with one root page and several intermidiate pages. A sketch for this could look like the following. For read information about an ID value we have to read 3 pages. It is the Root page, one Intermidiate page and the data page - instead of scanning all the data pages. Maybe only 3 pages even if we have many rows in the table and a scanning.

Root Page (1:78)	
Min value on the page	Page_id
1	1:87
13	1:88

Intermidiate Page (1:87)	
Min value on the page	Page_id
1	1:34
4	1:35
8	1:37

Intermidiate Page (1:88)	
Min value on the page	Page_id
13	1:66
24	1:47

In the next sketch we show a NonClustered Index on the column Firstname. The NonClustered Index contains two columns. The Key column and a reference to the ClusterKey value.

Key1 (Firstname)	ClusterKey
Ane	9
Anne	24
Bo	1
Bo	28
Carl	5
Dorthe	30
Finn	13
Gert	2
Hans	21
Karl	4
Maren	8
Nils	10
Nils	19
Nils	23
Ole	6
Pia	14
Tina	17

Depending on the number of rows and the size of the key value, the index is stored on one or more pages. If there are many pages, they are linked together as shown for the Clustered Index. Depending on the data in the index it can be structured in a B-Tree hierarchy.

When we search for Nils, we can see in the index that the 'first' Nils as the ClusterKey 10. The next Nils the ClusterKey 19 and the last ClusterKey 23. For each occurrence of Nils we have a Lookup/Seek in the Clustered Index with the ClusterKey value from the index if we want more columns than ID and Firstname. As seen, we jump around in the file(s) when performing Lookup. Therefore, the compiler may choose to ignore the

NonClustered Index and instead scan the Clustered Index combined with filtering. The compiler believes that this is faster and cheaper in terms of resources.

We can define a more effective index if we in the result want the columns ID, Firstname and Lastname. If we in the index add the column Lastname as shown following we can save the lookup. The Index is covered for the query because all the columns needed for the query is columns in the index. It will also be a covered index if it contains more columns than are needed, but very useful if the column being searched is the first column or simply because the index takes up significantly less space than the table. Key1 is Firstname, Key2 is Lastname and the ClusterKey is the column ID.

Key1 (Firstname)	Key2 (Lastname)	ClusterKey
Ane	Olsen	9
Anne	Andersen	24
Bo	Hansen	1
Bo	Thomsen	28
Carl	Petersen	5
Dorthe	Larsen	30
Finn	Knudsen	13
Gert	Jensen	2
Hans	Olsen	21
Karl	Christensen	4
Maren	Carlsen	8
Nils	Eriksen	10
Nils	Frandsen	19
Nils	Thomsen	23
Ole	Iversen	6
Pia	Didriksen	14
Tina	Olsen	17

If we are searching on a LastName value and we do not have a usable index, the compiler can scan the covered index above and then filter for the desired LastName value. The index is faster to Scan than the Clustered Index/table, where each row use 1800 bytes but an index row only 36 bytes in average.

Hopefully this small description about indexes helps to understand the operations seen in an execution plan. But last but not least, it is important to understand that the statement to be executed does not need to be changed, but the options given to the compiler/optimizer can improve the execution time. It is important to emphasize that creating indexes is a complex task and requires much more knowledge than this small overview provides. There can be a long way from understanding to using the possibility.

UNION, INTERSECT and EXCEPT

In SQL, it is possible to use the mathematical operations UNION, INTERSECT and EXCEPT. In some database systems EXCEPT is called MINUS. There are some simple rules for the operation. Both operands must have the same schema, and the result table will have the same schema as the operands. This means that if one of the operand tables has 5 columns, the other operand table must also have 5 columns. The result table has 5 columns, and the rows in the result are unique. We do not specify any conditions or DISTINCT,

These operations are very different from the JOIN operation, where one operand table can have 8 columns and the other 5 columns ending up with a result table with 13 columns. The join condition is important for the result. The join operation is binary. We cannot join three tables, but can join two tables given an intermidiate result. This result can be joined with the third table. Just as described under Join, it can be compared with adding three numbers. $3 + 5 + 2 = 8 + 2 = 10$. The precedence rule is from left to right. However, with an expression like $5 + 3 * 8 = 5 + 24 = 29$, some operations take precedence over others. Multiply/* is performed before addition/+.

For UNION, INTERSECT and EXCEPT the following precedents rules exists.

1. Expressions in parentheses
2. The INTERSECT operator
3. EXCEPT and UNION is evaluated from left to right.

The fact that the schema of the operand tables must be the same is called UNION compatibility. The term is used for all three operations, not only UNION but also for the INTERSECT and EXCEPT operations. The column names in the 2 tables may be different, but the names from the first SELECT statement are used for the result.

The system we use in the example is a small evening school where students may be enrolled in different courses. A course may be held over several semesters, and a student may be enrolled in several courses in the same semester. Only a minimal number of columns are included, and the results are displayed with ID values. Of course, different names should be displayed, but this is omitted to keep all statements simple and clear.

```sql
CREATE TABLE dbo.Student
(
        StudentID           INT             NOT NULL
                            CONSTRAINT PK_Student PRIMARY KEY,
        StudentName         VARCHAR (30)    NOT NULL
);

CREATE TABLE dbo.Course
(
        CourseID            INT             NOT NULL
                            CONSTRAINT PK_Course PRIMARY KEY,
        CourseName          VARCHAR (30)    NOT NULL,
        Semester            CHAR (6)        NOT NULL
);

CREATE TABLE dbo.StudentCourse
(
        StudentID           INT             NOT NULL
                            CONSTRAINT FK_StudentCourse_Student FOREIGN KEY REFERENCES dbo.Student (StudentID),
        CourseID            INT             NOT NULL
                            CONSTRAINT FK_StudentCourse_Course FOREIGN KEY REFERENCES dbo.Course (CourseID),
        CONSTRAINT PK_StudentCourse PRIMARY KEY (StudentID, CourseID)
);
GO
INSERT INTO dbo.Student (StudentID, StudentName) VALUES
        (11, 'Hanne'),      (12, 'Ib'),      (13, 'Karen'),      (14, 'Lis'),      (15, 'Ole'),
        (16, 'Per'),        (17, 'Knud'),    (18, 'Lars'),       (20, 'Alfred'),   (21, 'Louise');

INSERT INTO dbo.Course (CourseID, CourseName, Semester) VALUES
        (51, 'SQL', '022023'),      (52, 'Phyton', '022023'),
        (53, 'SQL', '012024'),      (54, 'Phyton', '012024'),
        (61, 'AI', '022024'),       (62, 'ChatGPT', '022024'),      (63, 'PowerBI', '022024');
```

```
INSERT INTO dbo.StudentCourse (StudentID, CourseID) VALUES
        (11, 52),   (11, 53),           (12, 51),   (12, 52),   (       13, 53),             (14, 51),   (14, 53),
        (15, 54),   (15, 53),           (16, 51),   (16, 52),   (       17, 51),   (17, 52),  (18, 51),   (18, 54);
```

The first example shows the UNION operation between two tables. It could be that two classes/courses are going to visit a company. To tell the company how many people are coming, a UNION operation is performed between the two courses. We use a UNION because the same student can be enrolled in both courses.

In the example, StudentID 12, 14, 16, 17 and 18 are taking the SQL course, and StudentID 11, 12, 16 and 17 are taking the Python course. There is overlap between the courses.

```
SELECT      StudentCourse.StudentID
            FROM dbo.StudentCourse INNER JOIN dbo.Course      ON StudentCourse.CourseID = Course.CourseID
            WHERE      CourseName = 'SQL'             AND
                       Semester = '022023'
UNION
SELECT      StudentCourse.StudentID
            FROM dbo.StudentCourse INNER JOIN dbo.Course      ON StudentCourse.CourseID = Course.CourseID
            WHERE      CourseName = 'Phyton'          AND
                       Semester = '022023';
```

The result is

StudentID
11
12
14
16
17
18

We can see that no condition is specified and duplicates are removed without specifying anything. That is the semantics of the operation. Both input tables have only one column and the result table has one column.

We can evaluate the result because there is a UNION ALL operation, This operation does not remove duplicates. Note that UNION and UNION ALL are two different operations. We do not use UNION ALL because this operation performs better than UNION, but because the task is to find out how many students visit the company.

```
SELECT      StudentCourse.StudentID
            FROM dbo.StudentCourse INNER JOIN dbo.Course      ON StudentCourse.CourseID = Course.CourseID
            WHERE      Course.CourseName = 'SQL'             AND
                       Course.Semester = '022023'
UNION ALL
SELECT      StudentCourse.StudentID
            FROM dbo.StudentCourse INNER JOIN dbo.Course      ON StudentCourse.CourseID = Course.CourseID
            WHERE      Course.CourseName = 'Phyton'          AND
                       Course.Semester = '022023';
```

StudentID
12
14
16
17
18
11
12
16
17

We have 9 StudentID values in the result. In the result from UNION there were only 6 different students. We can now tell the company that only 6 students and not 5 (from the SQL Course) + 4 (from the Phyton) Course = 9 students are coming to visit the company.

When planning exams, it is important to know if there are students who are enrolled in both courses and therefore cannot take the exam in both subjects at the same time. We can use INTERSECT for this operation.

```
SELECT      StudentCourse.StudentID
            FROM dbo.StudentCourse INNER JOIN dbo.Course    ON StudentCourse.CourseID = Course.CourseID
            WHERE    Course.CourseName = 'SQL'              AND
                     Course.Semester = '022023'
INTERSECT
SELECT      StudentCourse.StudentID
            FROM dbo.StudentCourse INNER JOIN dbo.Course    ON StudentCourse.CourseID = Course.CourseID
            WHERE    Course.CourseName = 'Phyton'           AND
                     Course.Semester = '022023';
```

The result is

StudentID
12
16
17

For exam planning, we can also choose to get an overview of which students only participate in the SQL course and which students only participate in the Python course. We use the EXCEPT operator. It is important to understand that UNION and INTERSECT are commutative, which means that the result will be the same regardless of whether we perform A UNION B or B UNION A. The same applies to INTERSECT. We know this from simple arithmetic, where 7 + 4 and 4 + 7 give the same result. The same applies to 5 * 8 and 8 * 5.

But 7 – 4 gives a different result than 4 – 7. This is also the case for the operation EXCEPT. The operation is not commutative. A EXCEPT B gives as a result all the rows from A that do not occur in B. The operation B EXCEPT A gives as a result all the rows in B that are not in A.

The first EXCEPT example returns SQL students who are not enrolled in the Python course.

```
SELECT      StudentCourse.StudentID
            FROM dbo.StudentCourse INNER JOIN dbo.Course    ON StudentCourse.CourseID = Course.CourseID
            WHERE    Course.CourseName  = 'SQL'             AND
                     Course.Semester    = '022023'
EXCEPT
SELECT      StudentCourse.StudentID
            FROM dbo.StudentCourse INNER JOIN dbo.Course    ON StudentCourse.CourseID = Course.CourseID
            WHERE    Course.CourseName  = 'Phyton'          AND
                     Course.Semester    = '022023';
```

This is the following students.

StudentID
14
18

The next EXCEPT example returns Python students who are not enrolled in the SQL course.

```
SELECT      StudentCourse.StudentID
            FROM dbo.StudentCourse INNER JOIN dbo.Course    ON StudentCourse.CourseID = Course.CourseID
            WHERE    Course.CourseName  = 'Phyton'          AND
                     Course.Semester    = '022023'
EXCEPT
SELECT      StudentCourse.StudentID
            FROM dbo.StudentCourse INNER JOIN dbo.Course    ON StudentCourse.CourseID = Course CourseID
            WHERE    Course.CourseName  = 'SQL'             AND
                     Course.Semester    = '022023';
```

StudentID
11

If we look at the operations above in another way we can see that. If we perform a UNION ALL between number 1, 2 and 3 we will as a result all student from number 4 of the following operations.

	Operation	Result StudentID
1	SQL INTERSECT Phyton	12, 16, 17
2	SQL EXCEPT Python	14, 18
3	Python EXCEPT SQL	11
4	SQL UNION Python	11, 12, 14, 16, 17, 18

We can use EXCEPT to find out if we have Students who have never enrolled in a course. These may need to be deleted. This kind of 'error' can occur in a system because a student must be created before a row can be inserted into the dbo.StudentCourse table. But what happens if the student never enrols in a course or the course is cancelled due to too few enrolees?

```
SELECT    StudentID
          FROM dbo.Student
EXCEPT
SELECT    StudentID
          FROM dbo.StudentCourse;
```

StudentID
20
21

We can also see if there are courses without any Students enrolled.

```
SELECT    CourseID
          FROM dbo.Course
EXCEPT
SELECT    CourseID
          FROM dbo.StudentCourse;
```

CourseID
61
62
63

We use the last statement to look at obvious improvements that of course should be included in the results table. No one can remember what CourseID = 52 is. In the first solution, we join with the dbo.Course table before the EXCEPT operation is performed. In the second example, we use a CTE. We execute first the join operation when the CourseID values are found.

```
SELECT    CourseID,
          CourseName
          FROM dbo.Course
EXCEPT
SELECT    StudentCourse.CourseID,
          Course.CourseName
          FROM dbo.StudentCourse INNER JOIN dbo.Course ON StudentCourse.CourseID = Course.CourseID;

WITH CourseWithoutStud
AS
(
SELECT    CourseID
          FROM dbo.Course
EXCEPT
SELECT    CourseID
          FROM dbo.StudentCourse
)
SELECT    Course.CourseID,
          Course.CourseName
          FROM CourseWithoutStud INNER JOIN dbo.Course ON CourseWithoutStud.CourseID = Course.CourseID;
```

The result is

CourseID	CourseName
61	AI
62	ChatGPT
63	PowerBI

The advantage of the last statement with CTE is that it is very easy to include more columns from the dbo.Course table. Maybe the result needs to be joined with more tables. Maybe the Course table may be joined with a table with the Location/Address of the course. If it is the Student table, the Address may need to be found by joining with a Zipinfo table, … All of those tables will be in a realistic system.

System Functions

There are a number of system Functions that must be used when extracting data from a table. These Functions are divided by the data type they have as input parameters and the data type that is returned. You may have heard of some of the Functions from other products, but the semantics in SQL Server are important to learn because they can differ from other systems.

The characteristic of a Function is that they

- May have input parameters, but not necessarily.
- Always returns one and only one value.
- Must be used in an expression.

In this chapter we will look at some of the most commonly used system functions and at the same time some functions that can be difficult to do without when solving a problem. Functions can be used when data needs to be returned in a specific form, or when conditions need to be specified in the WHERE clause. The functions are only described in general terms, so check the exact specification in the documentation.

I often hear that functions should be avoided, because they can cause poor performance. But of course they should only be used when necessary to solve a problem. There may be reasons why it is necessary to learn some different usage options and then choose the correct for the solution. However, it is also important to know how many times a Function is called. If we are going to use date/time from the system, it is not necessary to define a variable, assign the time to the variable by calling e.g. SYSDATETIME () and then use the variable in the WHERE clause. If SYSDATETIME () is used in the WHERE clause, it will only be called once. The result will be unpredictable if the function is called for each row and used to assess whether the row is from the correct day. It could change if the statement is executed before and after midnight, so that some rows are from one day and others from the next day.

- String-functions
    - LEFT, RIGHT and SUBSTRING
    - CONCAT
    - CHARINDEX
    - LTRIM, RTRIM and TRIM
    - UPPER and LOWER
- Numeric
    - ROUND
- Conversion
    - CAST
- Date and Time
    - YEAR
    - MONTH
    - DAY
    - DATEADD
    - DATEDIFF
    - DATEPART
    - GETDATE and SYSDATETIME
- NULL
    - ISNULL
    - COALESCE
    - NULLIF
- Logical
    - IIF

LEFT, RIGHT and SUBSTRING

LEFT returns the first characters of a string and RIGHT returns the last characters depending of the second parameter.

If we shorten a name where we have the columns Firstname and Lastname in a table and do not want to concatenate these in full length, as the name would then be too long, we can concatenate them in the following way

CONCAT (LEFT (Firstname, 1), '. ', Lastname)

Firstname	Lastname	Name
Ole	Olsen	O. Olsen
Ane Marie	Hansen	A. Hansen

SUBSTRING can replace LEFT and RIGTH but is used to extract data in the middle of a string. The first parameter is the string we extract the values from, the second parameter is the starting position and the last parameter is the number of characters to extract. If the starting position is greater than the length of the string, the empty string is returned and not NULL as maybe expected. In the example we have a string defined as CHAR (8) with a date in the format DDMMYYYY. All three parameters must be specified. In some systems the last parameter can be left out which mean that the string returned is from the start position and the rest of the string. It is allowed to have parameter values where the start + length is more than the length of string.

```
SELECT      Date,
            SUBSTRING (Date, 1, 2)      AS DD1,
            LEFT (Date, 2)              AS DD2,
            SUBSTRING (Date, 3, 2)      AS MM,
            SUBSTRING (Date, 5, 4)      AS YY1,
            RIGHT (Date, 4)             AS YY2
            FROM dbo.t;
```

Date	DD1	DD"	MM	YY1	YY2
26082024	26	26	08	2024	2024

CONCAT

With CONCAT, data with different data types can be concatenated. All columns are converted to a string before being concatenated. If a column is NULL, it is converted to the empty string. If we concatenated with the operator +/plus we must be sure that all columns are strings.

```
SELECT CONCAT (    Firstname, ' ', Lastname, ' - ', ID)                        AS CC,
                   Firstname + ' ' + Lastname + ' - ' + CAST (ID AS VARCHAR (5))   AS Plus
```

ID	Firstname	Lastname	CC	Plus
27	Ole	Hansen	Ole Olsen – 27	Ole Olsen – 27
44	NULL	Larsen	Larsen - 44	NULL

For the last row the column Plus is NULL because Firstname is NULL. If we have a column like Firstname that's allow NULL we must use the ISNULL or COALESCE function in the formula.

CHARINDEX

With CHARINDEX we can search for a string in another string. In the example we are searching for a comma in a Name because we want to change the order of Firstname and Lastname in a string and the Name is stored as 'Lastname, Firstname'. We can see that the comma is at position 9. Therefore Lastname ends at position 9 – 1 = 8. Firstname starts at position 9 + 1 = 10 or later. Maybe we didn't know whether the separator in the string is ',' or ', '. In the example a variable is used instead of a column.

```
DECLARE @Name          VARCHAR (30) = 'Petersen, Niels';

SELECT    CHARINDEX (',', @Name)                              AS CharPos,
          LEFT (@Name, CHARINDEX (',', @Name) - 1)            AS Lastname,
          SUBSTRING (@Name, CHARINDEX (',', @Name) + 1, 30)   AS Firstname;
```

Name	CharPos	Lastname	Firstname
Petersen, Niels	9	Petersen	Niels

The final result looks like this.

```
SELECT    @Name,
          CONCAT (
                  TRIM (SUBSTRING (@Name, CHARINDEX (',', @Name) + 1, 30)),
                  ' ',
                  LEFT (@Name, CHARINDEX (',', @Name) - 1)
                  )                    AS NewName;
```

Name	NewName
Petersen, Niels	Niels Petersen

LTRIM, RTRIM and TRIM

LTRIM removes leading/left spaces from a string. RTRIM moves trailing/right spaces. TRIM removes both leading and trailing spaces.

The first example shows the classic use of the LTRIM, RTRIM and TRIM functions. In the example, '<' and '>' is indicated before and after the result string to show what is being removed.

```
SELECT    CONCAT ('<', TRIM ('   Ole   '), '>')       AS Trim,
          CONCAT ('<', LTRIM ('   Ole   '), '>')      AS LTrim,
          CONCAT ('<', RTRIM ('   Ole   '), '>')      AS RTrim
```

Trim	LTrim	RTrim
<Ole>	<Ole >	< Ole>

TRIM is new in SQL Server and have new possibilities. It is possible to specify several characters to remove. In the example both '*' and '0' is removed. The syntax is

> TRIM ([LEADING | TRAILING | BOTH] [characters FROM] string)

The characters < and > are used to easily find out what has been removed.

```
SELECT    CONCAT ('<', TRIM (LEADING '0*' FROM '*******000000025'), '>')        AS LTrim,
          CONCAT ('<', TRIM (TRAILING ' ' FROM '000000025   '), '>')            AS RTrim,
          CONCAT ('<', TRIM (BOTH '0* ' FROM '*******000000025   '), '>')       AS Trim;
```

LTrim	RTrim	Trim
<25>	<000000025>	<25>

UPPER and LOWER

With UPPER, all letters are converted to uppercase and with LOWER, all letters are converted to lowercase. It could be used for Initials in an Employee table or for code values as Gendercode or car registration number.

```
SELECT    UPPER ('Knud')          AS Up,
          LOWER ('Christensen')   AS Low
```

ROUND

The function ROUND rounds a decimal value to the number of decimal places specified as parameter. Rounding up is done if the following digit in relation to the rounding is >= 5 else rounding down.

```
SELECT   ROUND (43.87, 0)                        AS Col1,
         ROUND (43.13, 0)                        AS Col2,
         ROUND (43.8765, 2)                      AS Col3,
         ROUND (43.7654, 2)                      AS Col4,
         ROUND (43.987654321, 2)                 AS Col5,
         ROUND (43.9876543210123456789, 6)       AS Col6
```

Col1	Col2	Col3	Col4	Col5	Col6
44.00	43.00	43.8800	43.7700	43.990000000	43.9876540000000000000

If we only want to display 2 decimal places for the last 2 columns, use the CAST function. This is described in the Conversion Functions review.

Conversion Functions

In this chapter, we look at the function CAST. There are several different conversion functions e.g. CONVERT, TRY_PARSE and TRY_CONVERT. CAST converts between data types and CONVERT to a specified format. The TRY versions of the functions is used to evaluate if a value can be converted.

CAST

CAST converts data from one data type to another data type. If the content cannot be converted to the specified data type, an error is returned.

In the first example, we look at the same data that was used by ROUND above. As you can see from the result, it is also rounded, but the resulting data type is well-defined based on the specification in CAST. ROUND preserves the original data type.

```
SELECT   CAST (43.87                  AS DECIMAL (11, 2))  AS Col1,
         CAST (43.13                  AS DECIMAL (11, 2))  AS Col2,
         CAST (43.8765                AS DECIMAL (11, 2))  AS Col3,
         CAST (43.7654                AS DECIMAL (11, 2))  AS Col4,
         CAST (43.987654321           AS DECIMAL (11, 2))  AS Col5,
         CAST (43.98765432101234      AS DECIMAL (11, 2))  AS Col6,
         CAST (43.9976                AS DECIMAL (11, 2))  AS Col7;
```

Col1	Col2	Col3	Col4	Col5	Col6	Col7
43.87	43.13	43.88	43.77	43.99	43.99	44.00

All conversions in the following statement can be performed without error. Note that DATE columns are given in different formats. The recommendation is to use the format yyyy-mm-dd. Col6 with REAL is rounded to 9.876543E+08, so digits 1 and 2 are rounded down, but Col7 is rounded up.

```
SELECT   CAST ('321005'       AS INT)         AS Col1,
         CAST ('123.45'       AS DECIMAL(9,3))  AS Col2,

         CAST ('20210811'     AS DATE)        AS Col3,
         CAST ('2021-08-11'   AS DATE)        AS Col4,
         CAST ('11-08-2021'   AS DATE)        AS Col5,
```

```
        CAST ('987654321'    AS REAL)         AS Col6,
        CAST ('987654399'    AS REAL)         AS Col7
```

Col1	Col2	Col3	Col4	Col5	Col6	Col7
321005	123.450	2021-08-11	2021-08-11	2021-11-08	9.876543E+08	9.876544E+08

The following statements returns an error.

```
SELECT    CAST ('43345'      AS SMALLINT)
```

Msg 244, Level 16, State 2, Line 202
The conversion of the varchar value '43345' overflowed an INT2 column. Use a larger integer column.

The error shows that there is an overflow for an INT2 data type. INT2 is SMALLINT - takes up 2 bytes.

```
SELECT    CAST ('20140229'   AS DATE)
```

Msg 241, Level 16, State 1, Line 203
Conversion failed when converting date and/or time from character string.

The year 2014 was not a leap year and February therefore only has 28 days.

YEAR, MONTH and DAY

The functions YEAR, MONTH, and DAY returns the year, month, and day from a column having one of the data types DATE, DATETIME or DATETIME2.

```
SELECT    YEAR ('2023-7-15')     AS Year,
          MONTH ('2023-7-15')    AS Month,
          DAY ('2023-7-15')      AS Day
```

Year	Month	Day
2023	7	15

DATEADD, DATEDIFF and DATEPART

With the DATEADD, DATEDIFF, and DATEPART functions calculations are performed on columns with one of the DATE, DATETIME, or DATETIME2 data types.

With DATEADD, the first parameter must specify which datepart to add

- For years we can specify YEAR, YY or YYYY
- For month we can specify MONTH, mm or m
- For days we can specify DAY, dd or d
- etc.

With DATEDIFF, the difference between two dates is calculated. Again, it must be stated at what level the calculation is to be made.

```
SELECT    DATEADD (DAY, 12, '2024-2-12')                        AS AddDay,
          DATEADD (MONTH, 12, '2024-2-12')                      AS AddMonth,

          DATEDIFF (YEAR, '2024-12-31', '2025-1-1')             AS DiffYear,
          DATEDIFF (MONTH, '2024-2-12', '2016-12-7')            AS DiffMonth,

          DATEPART (MINUTE, '2024-2-12 13:27:44.9876543')       AS PartMinute
```

AddDay	AddMonth	DiffYear	DiffMonth	PartMinute
2024-02-24 00:00:00.000	2025-02-12 00:00:00.000	1	-86	27

Note that the result of column DiffYear is 1, even though there is only one day between the dates. The formula used is

    YEAR ('2025-1-1') - YEAR ('2024-12-31')

Therefore, the calculation must be more complicated if we want to use the value to calculate interest.

There are only special functions for YEAR, MONTH and DAY. If we want to extract other parts from a date column, we use the DATEPART function. It could be HOURS, MINUTES, etc.

Never add an integer to a column with one of the date/time data types. It is allowed for the old data type DATETIME and the integer value is days.

SELECT   CAST ('2024-2-12' AS DATETIME) + 14 AS Plus14Days;

Plus14Days
2024-02-26 00:00:00.000

The following two statements will return an error because we are using one of the newer date data types. Asserting an integer will make it harder to convert to one of the newer date data types if we want to, because there are some advantages to these.

SELECT   CAST ('2024-2-12' AS DATE) + 14;

Msg 206, Level 16, State 2, Line 219
Operand type clash: date is incompatible with int

SELECT   CAST ('2024-2-12' AS DATETIME2) + 14;

Msg 206, Level 16, State 2, Line 220
Operand type clash: datetime2 is incompatible with int

GETDATE and SYSDATETIME

GETDATE () returns today's date and time. The data type of the return value is DATETIME. The function SYS-DATETIME () also returns today's date including time, but the data type of the return value is DATETIME2. Since these 2 functions have no input parameters, an empty parameter list must be specified with (). Use always SYSDATETIME () when you use the newer data type DATETIME2 and DATE.

        SELECT GETDATE (), SYSDATETIME ();

ISNULL and COALESCE

The ISNULL function takes two parameters. If the first parameter is NULL, the value of the second parameter is returned. If the second parameter is also NULL, NULL is returned.

SELECT   ISNULL (48, 99)   AS BothValue,
          ISNULL (NULL, 99)   AS FirstNULL,
          ISNULL (48, NULL)   AS LastNULL,
          ISNULL (NULL, NULL)   AS BothNULL

BothValue	FirstNULL	LastNULL	BothNULL
48	99	48	NULL

The return value has the same data type as the first parameter.

```sql
SELECT    ISNULL (CAST (48      AS SMALLINT), 99999)          AS BothValue
```

The statement return 48. The second parameter is not evaluated against the data type.

```sql
SELECT    ISNULL (CAST (NULL    AS SMALLINT), 99999)          AS FirstNULL
```

Msg 220, Level 16, State 1, Line 229
Arithmetic overflow error for data type smallint, value = 99999.

Because the first parameter is NULL with the data type SMALLINT, assigning 99999 to the return value will result in an error.

If we use a string column, we don't get an error, but the value of parameter 2 is truncated when it is returned.

```sql
SELECT    ISNULL (CAST (NULL AS VARCHAR (5)), 'We have an error')      AS FirstNULL
```

FirstNULL
We ha

Instead of the ISNULL function, we can use COALESCE. This function can take many parameters. It is the first parameter that is not NULL that is returned. COALESCE uses the datatype precedence rules, so there is no error if the parameters have different datatypes and the values can be converted to the chosen datatype. Using the data types SMALLINT and DATE together gives an error. Using SMALLINT, INT and BIGINT together is not a problem. The same for VARCHAR (5) and VARCHAR (10). If all parameters are NULL, NULL is returned.

```sql
SELECT    COALESCE (2, 4, 5)                          AS Col1,
          COALESCE (NULL, NULL, 3, NULL)              AS Col2,
          COALESCE (NULL, '234', 56)                  AS Col4,
          COALESCE (CAST (NULL AS SMALLINT), CAST (NULL AS INT), CAST (NULL AS BIGINT))      AS Col4,
          COALESCE (CAST (NULL AS DATE), CAST (NULL AS DATETIME), CAST (NULL AS DATETIME2))  AS Col5
```

Col1	Col2	Col4	Col4	Col5
2	3	234	NULL	NULL

Mix of the following data types return an error.

```sql
SELECT    COALESCE (CAST (NULL AS SMALLINT), CAST (NULL AS DATE))      AS Col1
```

Msg 206, Level 16, State 2, Line 234
Operand type clash: smallint is incompatible with date

IIF and NULLIF

The IIF function allows you to specify a condition for the result. If a column has a value instead of NULL, and you want to use the benefits of NULL, we can use IIF to convert the value to NULL.

From version 2022 we have the GREATEST and LEAST functions. If we have used a value instead of NULL, there is a problem using these functions. In the example, 99 is used instead of NULL.

We evaluate with the following table. For column m4, we insert 99 instead of NULL. When using data together with the GREATEST function, we must change 99 to NULL by using IIF or NULLIF.

```sql
CREATE TABLE dbo.Measures
(
        ID      INT     NOT NULL,
        m1      INT     NULL,
        m2      INT     NULL,
        m3      INT     NULL,
        m4      INT     NOT NULL
                CONSTRAINT DF_Measures_m4 DEFAULT (99)
);
```

With the first INSERT statement we insert values in all columns.

```sql
INSERT INTO dbo.Measures (ID, m1, m2, m3, m4) VALUES
        (1, 24, 56, 76, 11);

SELECT   GREATEST (m1, m2, m3, m4)                    AS AllValues,
         GREATEST (m1, m2, m3, IIF (m4 = 99, NULL, m4))   AS UseIIF,
         GREATEST (m1, m2, m3, NULLIF (m4, 99))       AS UseNULLIF
         FROM dbo.Measures;
```

AllValues	UseIIF	UseNULLIF
76	76	76

We don't have a problem. 76 is the largest value because IIF and NULLIF are used to change 99 to NULL in column m4 if the column is NULL. But in the example the value is 11.

If we insert the following row, column m4 will get the value 99 – the default value for the column - because m4 is not referenced in the INSERT statement.

```sql
INSERT INTO dbo.Measures (ID, m1, m2, m3) VALUES
        (2, NULL, 87, NULL);
```

The result after executing the above statement is

AllValues	UseIIF	UseNULLIF
99	87	87

For the column AllValues the default value/'fake NULL' is the GREATEST. For the column UseIIF we use the IIF function to change 99 to NULL for column m4, because we know, that this column has the DEFAULT. The GREATEST value is 87.

If DEFAULT value was 0, we will have a comparable problem with the LEAST function.

For the UseNULLIF column we use the function NULLIF. This function returns NULL if the two parameter values are equal. Both the function LEAST and GREATEST ignore NULL. The GREATEST is 87. NULLIF can be used if we not want the empty string in a column.

```sql
CREATE TABLE dbo.t
(
        ID              INT              NOT NULL,
        Txt             VARCHAR (100)    NULL,
        Integer         INT              NULL
);
```

For showing what happens when inserting a value

```sql
INSERT INTO dbo.t (ID, Txt, Integer) VALUES
        (1, 'Text', 27),
        (2, '', 0),
        (3, NULLIF ('', ''), NULLIF (0, 0)),
        (4, NULL, NULL);
```

The result is

ID	Txt	Integer
1	Text	27
2		0
3	NULL	NULL
4	NULL	NULL

If we want to clean data in a table, we can use NULLIF if NULL has been replaced by a value. It has been widely accepted for many years that a Data Warehouse and a Datamart must not have columns that can be NULL. I disagree with this. It's simple to change NULL to a value, but it can be difficult to figure out what replacement value has been used and will even depend on the data type, but NULL can be used for all data types. With NULL, some of the new functionality is not immediately usable.

Postscript

The reader of this book has hopefully been inspired to write basic SQL statements in a more systematic way and at the same time has seen the need to be careful, as there are many pitfalls.

It is important to evaluate the possibilities and learn if it is the right for own task. Many examples are shown on the Internet but not all are useful and not all fits with the world that you have and the database system you use.

It is important to understand the different operations and if we are practicing, even join of many tables is not so difficult. But use data that is created for evaluation, as it gives the opportunity to change the definition and thus learn about the possibility – is it important that a FOREIGN KEY is defined, what does it mean for the result if the column can be NULL or perhaps just make a correct calculation based on the data types chosen when the tables was created. Even standard systems are not well defined according to your world/domain.

Remember that we are often work with a system where it is not possible to change the definition. The responsible for the system will not allow just defining a lot of indexes.

There is a lot to learn if the focus is correctness.

I have published a book about writing manipulation statements. Since there are almost 1000 pages, it is divided into 3 physical books, but should be considered as one book. This book shows many details. SQL Server is used for all the examples. If another database system is used, many of the principles can be applied, but there may be details that need to be considered.

Applied SQL - Preparation of Manipulation Statements - SQL Server 2022.

Part 1 of 3 : How to Write SELECT in SQL Server
Part 2 of 3 : Different Objects and Index in SQL Server
Part 3 of 3 : Understanding How and Why in SQL Server